THE RAILWAY GROUPING 1923 TO THE BEECHING ERA

THE RAILWAY GROUPING 1923 TO THE BEECHING ERA

A New History

BOB PIXTON

AN IMPRINT OF PEN & SWORD BOOKS LTD.
YORKSHIRE – PHILADELPHIA

First published in Great Britain in 2024 by
Pen and Sword Transport
An imprint of
Pen & Sword Books Ltd.
Yorkshire - Philadelphia

Copyright © Bob Pixton, 2024

ISBN 978 1 39908 828 2

The right of Bob Pixton to be identified as Author of this work has been asserted by him in accordance with the Copyright, Designs and Patents Act 1988.

A CIP catalogue record for this book is available from the British Library.

All rights reserved. No part of this book may be reproduced or transmitted in any form or by any means, electronic or mechanical including photocopying, recording or by any information storage and retrieval system, without permission from the Publisher in writing.

Typeset in Palatino 11/13 by SJmagic DESIGN SERVICES, India.

Printed and bound in India by Parksons Graphics Pvt. Ltd.

Pen & Sword Books Ltd. incorporates the imprints of Pen & Sword Books: After the Battle, Archaeology, Atlas, Aviation, Battleground, Discovery, Family History, History, Maritime, Military, Naval, Politics, Railways, Select, Transport, True Crime, Fiction, Frontline Books, Leo Cooper, Praetorian Press, Seaforth Publishing, Wharncliffe and White Owl.

For a complete list of Pen & Sword titles please contact

PEN & SWORD BOOKS LIMITED
George House, Units 12 & 13, Beevor Street, Off Pontefract Road,
Barnsley, South Yorkshire, S71 1HN, England
E-mail: enquiries@pen-and-sword.co.uk
Website: www.pen-and-sword.co.uk

or

PEN AND SWORD BOOKS
1950 Lawrence Rd, Havertown, PA 19083, USA
E-mail: uspen-and-sword@casematepublishers.com
Website: www.penandswordbooks.com

CONTENTS

Acknowledgements		7
Chapter 1	Beginning	9
Chapter 2	Causes of the Grouping	13
Chapter 3	Pre-Grouping Amalgamations	20
Chapter 4	The Grouping	22
Chapter 5	Personalities	30
Chapter 6	The Early Years	32
Chapter 7	The Economic Conditions After the Grouping	39
Chapter 8	Railway Finances	42
Chapter 9	Electrification Schemes	58
Chapter 10	The Rise of Cars and Lorries	67
Chapter 11	Trainspotting	70
Chapter 12	Post-Grouping Innovation	72
Chapter 13	Coping with Heavier Trains	76
Chapter 14	Streamlined Engines	89
Chapter 15	England's First Streamlined Train	94
Chapter 16	Rivalry in the High Speed Era of the 1930s	97
Chapter 17	Engines Touring Abroad	103
Chapter 18	Camping Coaches	107
Chapter 19	Excursions and Holidays in the 1920s and 1930s	109
Chapter 20	Named Trains in the Post-Grouping Years	132
Chapter 21	1930s Stories That Weren't Happy Endings	137

Chapter 22	Line Closures Before Dr Beeching	138
Chapter 23	London Transport Board	141
Chapter 24	New Engines Built During the 1940s	145
Chapter 25	Effects of the War on the Railways	154
Chapter 26	The Legacy of the Grouping	180
Chapter 27	The Eventful 1950s	188
Chapter 28	Standardisation of Railway Locomotives	194
Chapter 29	The Rise of the Motor Car, Package Holidays and Motorways	198
Chapter 30	BR's Modernisation Plan	202
Chapter 31	New Diesel Locomotives	209
Chapter 32	The Arrival of Dr Beeching	218
Select Bibliography		221
Glossary		222
Index		224

Flying Scotsman '100 not out'.

ACKNOWLEDGEMENTS

First thanks must go to the staff at Pen & Sword for not only encouraging me to put this volume together but for their support during its gestation. Many thanks must go to Peter Todd who, with his extensive knowledge on all things railway, was able to cast an eye over the material. In this electronic age I would have sunk if it had not been for the 'IT support' of Jonathan Harrison; much gratitude. I am indebted to Dr Rosa Matheson for her support and perspective regarding the changing role of women during, and in between, both world wars. The normal references to public libraries and other repositories of maps, plans etc. is sadly lacking due to the time when this book was written, due to restrictions

Non-stop water, 1950s. Water troughs were not a new feature on the main lines. By these devices, the engine's tender could have its water refilled without the train needing to stop at a station. This saved valuable time not only for the competitive nature of express trains but also enabled turnaround times to be reduced, leading to better utilisation of platform space. Here, Castle Class engine No. 5084 *Reading Abbey* is racing over the water troughs on the main line near Goring in the Thames Valley, probably a little faster than the 45mph ideal speed. Note the name-boards on the carriage roofs. Drainage from the spray (apart from soaking the unwary passengers in the first few compartments) could unsettle the ballast the sleepers and rails were on unless culverts were adequate. Often horizontal sleepers were laid next to the troughs to mitigate against this effect. (BPC)

Which system? This is the platform end at Sutton station in the late 1920s. Entering is a passenger train behind a steam engine. On the right, at ground level can be seen the live electric line of the third rail system, at 650VDC. Meanwhile, up above the train can be made out the steelwork carrying wires energised at 6.7kVAC. In the end it was the third-rail system that persists, even to this day. (Lens of Sutton)

imposed by the Covid pandemic. The same must be said about personal contacts which were restricted to telephone and e-mail communications due to the circumstances at the time.

Begging Your Indulgence

Many of my previous works have been of the line history type. This volume is totally different. With such a wide ranging title, over a long time span not withstanding some of the economic conditions encountered, the availability of (any) photographic evidence has been sparse to say the least. Consequentially, I have had to use what I could find, sometimes this has led to me including materials that stray outside the time period to illustrate an idea. I have done this with the maxim that in an illustrated book, no picture is not good and a picture, with a little leeway, is better. So, please, when you are reading a chapter, if a picture seems out of place, it is because that is as good as it gets.

CHAPTER 1
BEGINNING

For many people with no particular interest in railways or historical events in general, the thirty year period between 1925 to 1955 were just the same as the similar time frame, say, from 1890 to 1920. In railway terms, nothing could be further from the truth.

During the latter period, in many respects the railways were contracting. However, there were very large forces in society that impacted on what the railways did. Some would say that the employment of women fundamentally altered the structure of our society in a way that cannot be reversed. Another great influence was the replacement of the horse and cart by cars, vans and lorries, again in a non-reversible way. Possibly the greatest social change that incurred in the latter period, which shows no sign of abating, is the development of leisure time, including holidays. Never before have so many people had so much 'free' time or travelled so much both at home and abroad. If there is one thing that railways excel at it is in bulk transportation, be it coal, ores, finished goods or people. Without this capability it is doubtful that we would have

Football supporters. While these happen to support Arsenal, a North London club, their numbers could be in Newcastle, Manchester, Birmingham and several other clubs in London. Apart from a few clubs like Manchester United (from 1935) and West Bromwich, who had Hawthorns Halt station (1931) most football clubs did not have dedicated trackside platforms. Nevertheless, most supporters either walked or travelled by bus or train, especially in urban areas. Mass movement to sporting events would have been almost impossible without trains to transport people. (BPC)

Motor van. Many people think that it was the motor car, in all its shapes and forms, that 'did for the railways'. The intrusion of motorised vehicles into all forms of transport started well before the Grouping. This van belongs to the Lancashire and Yorkshire Railway (L&YR), destined to become part of the London, Midland and Scottish Railway (LMSR) from 1922. This would have replaced horse and cart transport in many towns and cities. (R.K. Blencowe)

emerged victorious from worldwide conflicts – twice. While in the earlier period railways were expanding at an ever-increasing rate, it is my contention that they were increasing the magnitude of what railways did, not the range of things they did.

Perhaps I am missing the point and it was the effect of two world wars that led to the biggest changes on how society operates. So, what was so special about this latter period, incorporating the Grouping? To many onlookers, this period of time was the interregnum between two world wars and is epitomised by streamlined trains and records.

It was a great deal more than this. Sure, there were problems resulting from the conflict, the enforced merger of railway companies into the Big Four, and the downturn in world economic activity. However, some companies, under dynamic leadership, not only got on with the job but led their workforce to produce world leading networks and layouts. Others, after burying the hatchet, went on to produce record breaking services. All this with the threat of motor vehicles in the background – three remarkable decades indeed.

Given all this positivity, it would be tempting to think that the Grouping was a roaring success. However, there were gloomy economic conditions on the horizon. Readers may think the railways sank into a dark age but little could be further from the truth. There were tough conditions ahead but due to government foresight, and some would say due to the Grouping itself, the late 1920s and the 1930s were times of great forward looking railway enterprise. It was not all fast passenger trains either. Most railway companies' revenue came from the movement of goods, especially coal and ores. However, as much of the movement of goods occurred at night, it was infrequently observed by the public.

Paddington station, 1930s. The Great Western Railway (GWR) had a vibrant publicity department, and it was from there that these two names probably emerged. Hanging about on the Lawn at Paddington station whilst waiting for a tea-time departure, this scene could be captured. On the right is the 4.00 pm arrival from Aberystwyth as the Cambrian Coast Express with a motor coach on the wide cab-road. No sooner had its passengers departed and the train to the left arrived. The Bristolian had, apart from a stop at Bath, sprinted non-stop to arrive here at 4.05 pm. The large reporting numbers on the engines' smoke boxes were meant to help signalmen identify trains and this was inaugurated by the GWR in the late 1930s. (BPC)

This view of the country's railways incorporates how they managed after the First World War, during the economic conditions of the 1930s, the prelude to the Second World War and under government control, again. The immediate enthusiasm following the Grouping resulted in the British Empire Exhibition, followed by celebrations for the centenary of steam. Hard on their heels were comparative trials between companies' locomotives, the 'Great Exchanges', tracked by the hype and publicity of an American tour of the Royal Scot. However, this euphoria was short lived when the whole country's efforts were concentrated on conflict and repairs to the system. Following the peace was the realisation that a state run, and controlled, system was in the country's best interest, leading to nationalisation.

Of course, all stories have an ending. Where should this one be? I have chosen the end of the 1950s. The Grouping had long gone and its effects (nationalisation) too with is legacy, the Modernisation Plan of 1955, was announced. It was probably the time when politicians started to look seriously at the railway system and tried to manage it. Until then, commercial views had always held sway, so it was the end of an era, as well as leading to the decline of steam. In perspective there was the Beeching era, financial targets and the selling off of the railways back to private companies again.

I have tried to select features that exemplify how the railways coped with the forced amalgamations imposed upon them by the government and the forward-looking spirit embodied by the Big Four and their successor, British Railways (BR). Given the limited space this illustrative compilation is not exhaustive nor all-embracing, simply cases to show how the railways managed, and expanded, in no particular order, quasi chronological. Given the vast range of examples to show the railways during this period of time, I have had to be selective and so I may have omitted many good cases – c'est la vie.

12 • THE RAILWAY GROUPING 1923 TO THE BEECHING ERA

Coronation of Queen Elizabeth II, 1953.
The biggest event of the decade has to be the Coronation of Queen Elizabeth II in 1953. Every village and community held some sort of celebration, and it seemed that half the population descended on London to get a look at the procession. With clogged roads, the only way to get about was by the crowded Tube – railways at their best. A coronation mug – remember these? All primary aged children were given one. I dropped mine, and it broke, on the way home from school – what happened to yours? (BPC)

CHAPTER 2
CAUSES OF THE GROUPING

All good stories have a backstory and the Grouping is no exception. Following the end of the Edwardian period and well into the reign of King George V, railways seemed to be on the crest of a wave. The country itself was confident, ambitious, audacious and yet within just over a decade this was all to change. What happened?

A Great War

In the early years of the twentieth century, the country had around 120 railway companies, 23,000 miles of rail track and 4,000 stations. Passenger numbers were on an upward trend having reached dizzying heights. The railway had become one of Britain's biggest employers with more than 700,000 workers. About 13,000 women worked on the railway in 1914, mostly in domestic jobs such as cleaning, washing and waitressing. Many claimed Britain had the best railways in the world at this period, and it could certainly be justified.

The railways had surpassed all other forms of transport in the country. In 1905, one company, the GWR, carried more freight than all the inland water ways of the country put together. Britain was in an economic boom and the railways were well placed to capitalise on this. By 1912, freight tonnage had trebled since 1870 and passenger numbers had quadrupled.

Just after the start of the new king's reign – George V ascended to the throne in 1910 – the Railway Executive Committee (REC) was formed to liaise between the War Office and some of the railway companies. Planning had been ongoing, as in 1911 plans were produced in the 'War Book' for the embarkation of men and materials, chiefly from ports such as Southampton, for the Continent. Even that was foreseen by legislation in 1871 so a lot of planning for a European war had occurred before the outbreak of the First World War. The conflict, when it happened, was never thought of as being one that would last, 'it will be over by Christmas' was the often quoted saying. This pervaded throughout government thinking and so long term planning did not happen and any other workings, lack of maintenance and financial issues would be sorted out soon after. There was no need to get flustered.

Railways and The First World War

The operations of the REC were, in perspective, the forerunner of not only the Grouping but nationalisation many years later. The railway companies, instead of operating individually for profit, were obliged to co-operate and work in the national interest. As well as their normal business, the railways had to transport munitions,

Air raid. Bomb damage at Scarborough. As the risk from air raids was unexpected, there were no government plans for the evacuation of the civilian population. The government tried to warn people when an attack was coming to keep them safe. (BPC)

armaments and troops at a time when their manpower was being reduced due to call-up and much rolling stock being commandeered to transport materials for the war effort. To discourage passenger traffic, fares were increased, duplicated services merged, and freight wagons were 'pooled' to reduce light loads.

Air raids over the UK during the First World War were sporadic and relatively small scale until late 1916 when the Imperial German Air Service formed the 'England Squadron' designed to break the fighting spirit of the British people. A twelve-month campaign, beginning with a raid on Folkestone in May 1917, saw the squadron's Gotha heavy bombers, and later the giant bombers conduct fifty-two raids across the country, leaving 836 dead and 1,982 wounded. These bombing missions intensified the long-range attacks delivered by Zeppelin airships – the hydrogen-filled, commercial balloons converted to carry a 2-ton payload of bombs. At 11,000ft, Zeppelins could turn off their engines, drifting silently to carry out surprise attacks, however inaccurate the mission was. They also raised the final death toll for the war to 1,413, according to official statistics published in January 1919.

No one expected air raids, so when German airships first flew over Britain, the country was unprepared. The worst raid in terms of casualties took place on 13 June 1917 when twenty Gotha bombers attacked London; 162 were killed and 432 injured. Particularly traumatic was the death of schoolchildren; a bomb struck Upper North Street School in Poplar, killing eighteen young children. On 7 July, a further daylight raid resulted in fifty-seven civilian deaths, prompting public anger and newspaper reports about the lack of warning and absence of effective defences. Targeted on the civilian population rather than military sites, these aerial attacks emphasised the random quality of warfare. Out of the blue, anyone living in a town or port within range of bombers and airships could lose their life. The outrage exhibited by many citizens (Zeppelins were described in British propaganda as 'the baby-killer') was akin to the feelings expressed by Londoners in the aftermath of the 7/7 bombings when ordinary people travelling

Rail sidings, New Cross. Although there were air raids during the First World War, killing around 1,500 civilians, there was little impact on the railway system. Railways showed remarkable resilience and an ability to absorb damage- very soon things were put right and normal service was restored. Airships were particularly vulnerable to attack both from aircraft and also from ground-based weapons. Consequently, they had to fly at higher altitudes diminishing the accuracy of their bombs. (BPC)

to work were suddenly struck down without warning. The bombing raids were not accurate, but they still caused death and damage. In times to come, whistles would sound the alarm and people learnt to run for cover in the Underground or at home in cellars. By autumn 1917, eighty-six Tube stations had been made available as public shelters with a capacity of 250,000. Rules to govern behaviour and control numbers were regulated by Special Constables. It was estimated that the number of civilians taking shelter in the Tube approached a peak of 300,000, whilst a further 500,000 were thought to be using basements and cellars for protection during raids. The increase in German air raids was one of the reasons the Royal Air Force (RAF) was subsequently formed in April 1918. Britain needed better aircraft and more trained pilots.

Streetlights were dimmed so enemy pilots would struggle to see their targets and whistles were blown to raise the alarm. Searchlights helped gunners to spot airships or planes and shoot them when they were close. Policemen shouted warnings as they cycled round the streets wearing a sign saying, 'take cover'. The aerial campaign of 1917–18 was designed to break the morale of the British people. In this respect, it failed as there was no sustained public campaign to call the war to a halt. Nevertheless, the raids had a significant impact on behaviour. Not only did they cause outrage, but the attacks also created fear in areas of London repeatedly subjected to bombing. Without a warning system that allowed civilians sufficient time to move to shelters and delays in setting up anti-aircraft batteries and fighter defences, it took time for people to work out the risks and ways to defend themselves.

Concerned by the number of civilians who had sought shelter in the Underground during the First World War, in 1924 the government set up an Air-Raid Precautions Sub-Committee of the Committee of Imperial Defence. In the belief that ordinary people who had no military training would not be able to withstand the mental and physical demands of sustained aerial bombardment, it concluded that 'the moral effect of air attack is out of all proportion to the material effect'. The secretary of the subcommittee argued that victory in any future war 'will rest with that country whose people will endure bombardment the longer with greater stoicism'. He questioned the preparedness of the general public 'who have no realisation what is in store in the event of another war on a large scale, and I am apprehensive that the full realisation would come as so great a shock that general panic would ensue'. As a result, the primary aim of the ARP, as defined years later, was not the protection of individuals and property from destruction, but 'the maintenance of the morale of the people'. Plans were laid for some 17,000 regular troops and 20,000 reserve constables to be drafted into London to control the expected mass exodus from London, and to prevent panic at main line stations and entrances to the Tube.

The Role of the Railways

One thing the railways are excellent at performing is the mass movement of goods and people. From the beginning of the First World War, the British naval fleet was based at Scapa Flow, in the Orkney Isles. Rail was then the only transport capable of moving large numbers of passengers, but the timetabled services were unable to cope with the additional flow required by the fleet. In 1917, Admiral John Jellicoe ordered the naval train to run the 717 miles from London to Thurso daily, the longest regular scheduled service in UK railway history. The train is credited with carrying 475,000 people between February 1917 and April 1919 as well as carrying the fleet's mail. Taking twenty-two hours, several refreshment stops were required en route. The 'Jellicoe Express' service transported Royal Navy personnel from London Euston to Thurso, where they travelled on to the Scapa Flow naval base in Orkney. Forsinard was the penultimate stop before Thurso, and it was where the engines would stop to take on additional water. As well as servicemen, there were special trains carrying coal to fuel the fleet.

Opposite above: **London and North Western Railway (LNWR) coal train.** South Welsh coal was the best for naval purposes and so it, rather than the inferior products of closer fields, would be sent to Scapa Flow. A plaque has been unveiled at Crewe station in Cheshire to recognise the vital role played by a Royal Navy train. Crewe station, one of the few scheduled stops on the 717-mile twenty-one hour and thirty minute journey. The train was named after Admiral John Jellicoe, who commanded the Grand Fleet at the Battle of Jutland in 1916. Crewe served as a welcome refreshment stop, where over 300 women volunteers worked around the clock to provide refreshments in a canteen on Platform 6. Travelling on it was usually a nightmare – invariably overcrowded, most passengers were unlikely to get a seat, and only the shortest of them could hope to get any sleep (if they could find an empty wire luggage rack). During the First World War it left London at 6.00 pm, arriving at Thurso at 3.30 pm the following day. The southbound service took an hour longer, and the express also served as a convenient link to Rosyth Dockyard on the Firth of Forth. Naturally, pictures are rare. (BPC)

Opposite below: **The Call Up.** The appetite of the Western Front was such that this was not enough. Consequently, single men between the ages of 18 and 41 were called up from 1916. Later this was amended to include married men, and those aged under 41. Across the British Isles, some 16,000 men claimed conscientious objection. The vast majority did so on religious grounds. Only a minority were political opponents of the war, and they generally received harsher treatment. Military tribunals had the power to exempt people from active military service. The tribunals might recommend a non-combatant role in the armed forces, for example in a medical unit, or alternative civilian work such as forestry, factory, social or hospital work and, towards the end of the war, coal mining. Those men who would not accept this compromise were known as Absolutists, as they demanded absolute exemption. They would accept no compromise with the army, would not serve in uniform in a non-combatant role and as a result were imprisoned for two years with hard labour. Posing in front of a 'call to arms' poster in Todmorden are the nation's young men, eager to give the Hun a bloody nose and be back by Christmas. It is hard for us to appreciate the enthusiasm that the enlisting generated. (BPC)

CAUSES OF THE GROUPING • 17

Women filling the gaps. Women at work in a factory at Doncaster. With 100,000 men from the railways enlisted, women stepped in to fill essential functions. In fact, more than 1.6 million women took on traditionally male jobs, with more than 100,000 working in various forms of transport, particularly as engineers. Many remained in their new positions at the end of the war. The number of women working on the railway has never fallen below pre-First World War levels. Many roles on the railways were performed by women, often clerical. The role of women in securing victory cannot be underestimated; indeed, one of the reasons that Germany lost the war in 1918 was that it never succeeded in fully mobilising its female population. There were far reaching consequences to mobilising the country's women into work. It is commonly thought that women went into factories. However, when the introduction of military conscription after the war clearly wasn't over by Christmas, it became vital to mobilise women to fill the gaps in the factories, fields, transport and other essential areas. In the fields, the Women's Land Army employed over 260,000 women as farm labourers, a vital role as Allied merchant ships bringing supplies from overseas were being menaced by German U-boats at sea. Women living in the country were also encouraged to work together to grow and preserve food. In 1915, branches of the Women's Institute (WI) were set up across the UK. The first WI meeting in Britain took place at Llanfairpwllgwyngyll on Anglesey, North Wales on 16 September 1915. Another area where large numbers of women were employed was transport. Women worked as conductresses (and occasionally drivers) on buses, trams and Underground trains. The women who volunteered to work in industry were often sent some distance from home. There was great debate about the effect of this type of work on the morality of young women, particularly as many were away from their parents for the first time in their lives, and they had money from their wages to spend. However, there was a downside to employing women in munitions factories. In addition, many suffered ill health from the chemicals with which they worked. They were often nicknamed 'canaries' because of their yellow skin, caused by exposure to TNT. Around 400 women died from overexposure to TNT during the First World War. (BPC)

More than 100,000 men who worked on the railways, enlisted when war broke out, leading to a substantial skills shortage at home when the railway was under great pressure to deliver forces and supplies to the front line. When Britain declared war on Germany in 1914, trains efficiently moved huge numbers of troops and equipment between the Home Front and France. Trains also transported rations, water and coal across Britain and Continental Europe in a way not previously possible during conflict.

Railway workshops. Although scattered about the country, there were many premises that could be adapted. Ideally placed, these large sites turned their attention to making armaments; repairing locomotives and wagons would have to wait. At the end of the war, the social fabric that existed in 1914 had been shattered in such ways that it would never be the same again. Not surprisingly, at the end of the war railway companies were given back a system in poor shape, depleted of manpower and with a financial situation that had deteriorated. Improvements, if any, were going to be a long way in the future. (BPC)

CHAPTER 3
PRE-GROUPING AMALGAMATIONS
THE TASTE OF THINGS TO COME

Two pre-Grouping amalgamations will be looked at in detail in this chapter. One point of view is that these companies, and others, were pre-emptive, joining forces to give themselves a head start in case of future problems and to prevent other companies getting in the way of their preferred partner.

London and North Western Railway (LNWR), and Lancashire and Yorkshire Railway (L&YR)

As the Transport Act 1921 provided the writing on the wall for the unison of the railway companies in two years' time, these two companies chose a more suitable time for themselves – 1922. Since 1905, there had been close co-operation between the two companies in inter-changeability of tickets, goods collection and delivery. The First World War had

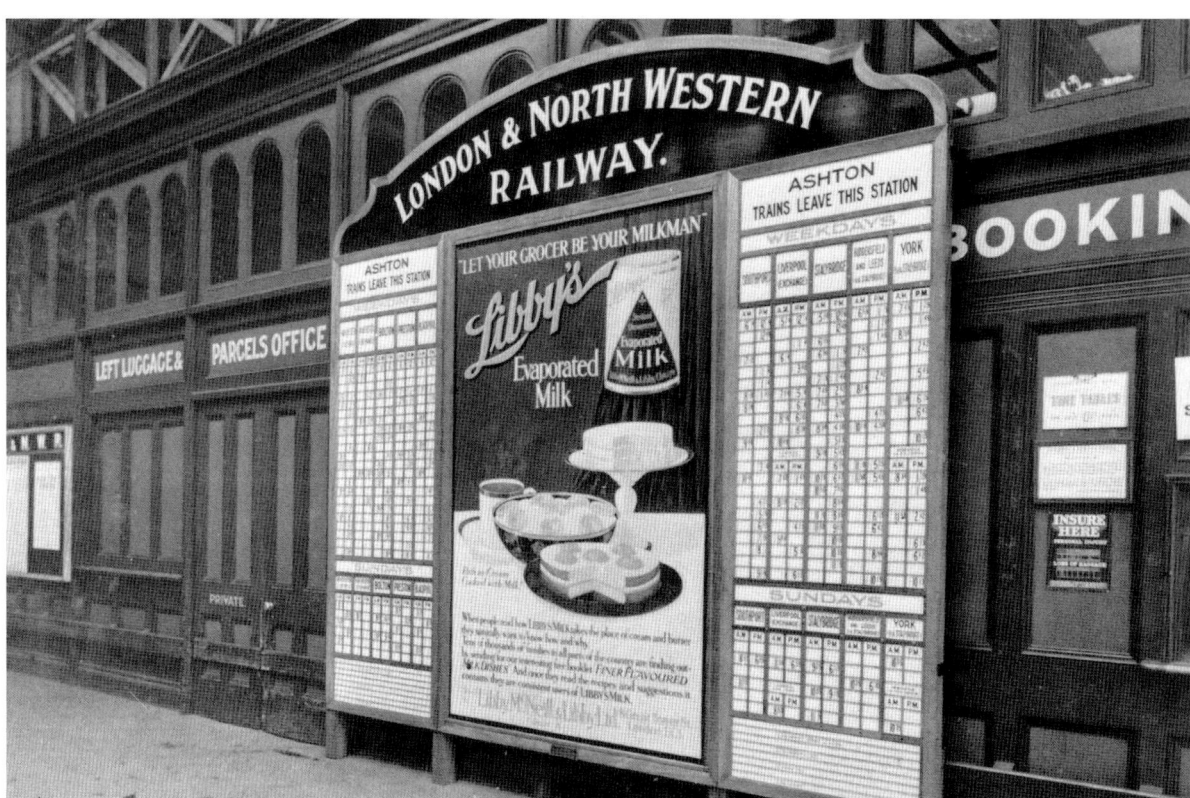

1922. This is the departure board at Ashton-under-Lyne, L&YR territory to the east of Manchester. This photograph was taken in 1922, a year before the official Grouping. (BPC)

left both companies short of quality managers and were often referred to as the London, Midland and Northern Group – they saw the sense in closer working relationships as a prelude to the merger which had to be completed in January 1923. With the Midland also entering into the fray at that time, perhaps this pre-emptive strike was to head off what to be a tussle within the LMSR. Some would say that its effects hampered the new company by five years compared to amalgamations that were relatively free from the in-house arguments.

The Hull and Barnsley Railway (H&BR) as part of the North Eastern Railway (NER), 1922–23

The Railways Act 1921 ended H&BR's independence, and on 1 April 1922 they became part of the NER. The locomotive works at Springhead was downgraded – the extent of locomotive maintenance was reduced, and the carriage works closed, skilled workers and machinery were relocated to Darlington. Due to a number of duplications with the station names, some were renamed; Howden (H&BR) became Howden South, and Eastrington (H&BR) became Eastrington North with Eastrington (NER) becoming Eastrington South.

Incorporation into the NER was just part of a larger scale of consolidation throughout the British railway system, and on 1 January 1923 the NER, along with the Hull and Barnsley line, became part of the London and North Eastern Railway (LNER). Whilst the NER concentrated on heavy industry in the North East, the main priority for the H&BR was rooted in the movement of coal from pit to port. Hull was also an important port for the landing and dispatching of fish. With both industries having different demands, their combination was a foretaste of what was to happen the next year.

Cannon Street station, Hull, date unknown. This was the passenger terminus of the Hull, Barnsley and West Riding Junction Railway and Dock Company, which was rebranded in 1905 as the Hull and Barnsley Railway. It opened on 27 July 1885. The station was planned as a goods station only, and the passenger terminus should have been built 0.25 miles south on Charlotte Street. Lack of funds meant that Cannon Street station had to serve both functions. Passenger services were provided in a converted building originally intended as a carriage shed. This was the company's main station in the city. The photographer is standing on Cannon Street looking at the main buildings with its name between the windows. The person walking along the pavement has just passed an entrance to the goods yard and is passing, on his right, the passenger entrance to the station. It closed just after the Grouping in 1924, after the LNER had built the Spring Bank chord. Note the complete absence of cars and lorries. (BPC)

CHAPTER 4
THE GROUPING

Following their golden era, the railways rose to the occasion during the First World War with their divisions put aside. The economic effects of the war were devastating to British industry, none more so than the railways. By the end of the war, 20,000 railway staff had tragically lost their lives; few industries could lose that number from its workforce without it having a dramatic effect of its performance. The railway remembers them in memorials across the country. All photographs in this chapter are courtesy of BPC.

War memorial, York. This memorial is in York, adjacent to the city wall. One of the first railway companies to arrive in the city punctured the old city wall to have their station closer to the city centre. (BPC)

Government Control

The numerous railway companies had been put under the umbrella of a government body, the REC, which effectively ran the business. The general manager of the NER, Alexander Butterworth, became the chairman of the REC too, until 1919.

When the First World War ended and the system was handed back to its former owners, it needed repair, the engines were worn out and the industry in chaos. The Liberal government of the day was faced with a national catastrophe and so proposed to nationalise the system. It is tempting to hold the superficial view that since the Grouping followed the First World War, that one is the cause of the other. At the end of the war, the government repaid to the railway companies a sum of money that the railways could have been expected to have earned in the intervening period of the war. While most students of railway history will have no difficulty in answering the pub quiz question, 'Why is 1 January 1923 a significant date?' they would be hard pushed to say when the process started. If one expected government control of the railways to start the day war broke out, 2 August 1914, then one fails to grasp the size and scale of the undertaking.

After the war, it was generally agreed that to move forward, the railways could not revert to the situation that existed before the war. Whilst nationalisation had been in the background (ever since the 1830s) it found little favour with the railway companies themselves and the government. Indeed, the public were in favour of retaining time honoured names such as Caledonian, Cambrian and Midland. However, the reality of the situation was that certain lines would have gone bankrupt had it not been for the principle that providing the overall system made a profit, the profitable lines could support the less viable ones to ensure the survival of a larger network. A half way-house compromise was produced, on 7 June 1920 when nationalisation was abandoned at a cabinet meeting, and on 19 August 1921 the Railways Act received the Royal Assent and again on 1 January 1923 when the legislation came into force. Thus, when the 'Grouping' happened, the railways had been under some form of government control for many years. The Railways Act 'grouped' (most) of the railway companies into one of the four big companies (the Big Four), GWR, LMSR, LNER and SR, being, roughly geographically centred. This was not the only plan to organise the country's railways. Others suggested all lines north of the border into a Scottish railway and others proposed various amalgamations in Devon and Cornwall. Another suggested the Great Central Railway (GCR), the Midland Railway (MR) and the Glasgow and the South Western Railway (G&SWR) all merging. For a variety of different reasons, the plan that was agreed upon envisaged four companies, SR, GWR, LNER and LMSR although there was a considerable overlap in some areas, notably Cornwall, Wales and parts of Scotland. Who could say that a 'Big Six' set of railway companies would have been better for the country and their shareholders? Interestingly, the ex-LMSR takeover of the former GCR's London extension and the emergence of a Scottish region under BR illustrating what could have happened with hindsight. The formation of the LMSR has been cited as a result of 'a merger that nobody wanted' in some circles.

Outside the Grouping

There were some organisations that were joint railways, such as the Midland and Great Northern Joint Railway (M&GNJR), and they remained separate and not aligned to any of the Big Four.

The Somerset and Dorset Joint Railway (S&DJR). This map shows one such railway, the S&DJR was well liked by rail enthusiasts. This line links Bath (and its Midlands connections), with Bournemouth in the south. There was also a branch to the west to the Somerset coast at Burnham and Bridgewater. I well remember travelling on the line's most famous train, the Pines Express from Gloucester Eastgate to Manchester Mayfield (Manchester London Road was being renovated to become Piccadilly). Carrying a suitcase on the long footbridge between Gloucester's two stations (Central for GWR trains from my home in Swindon and Eastgate for MR and the Pines Express). Having performed this feat there were several hours perched on a suitcase in the corridor to look forward to. (BPC)

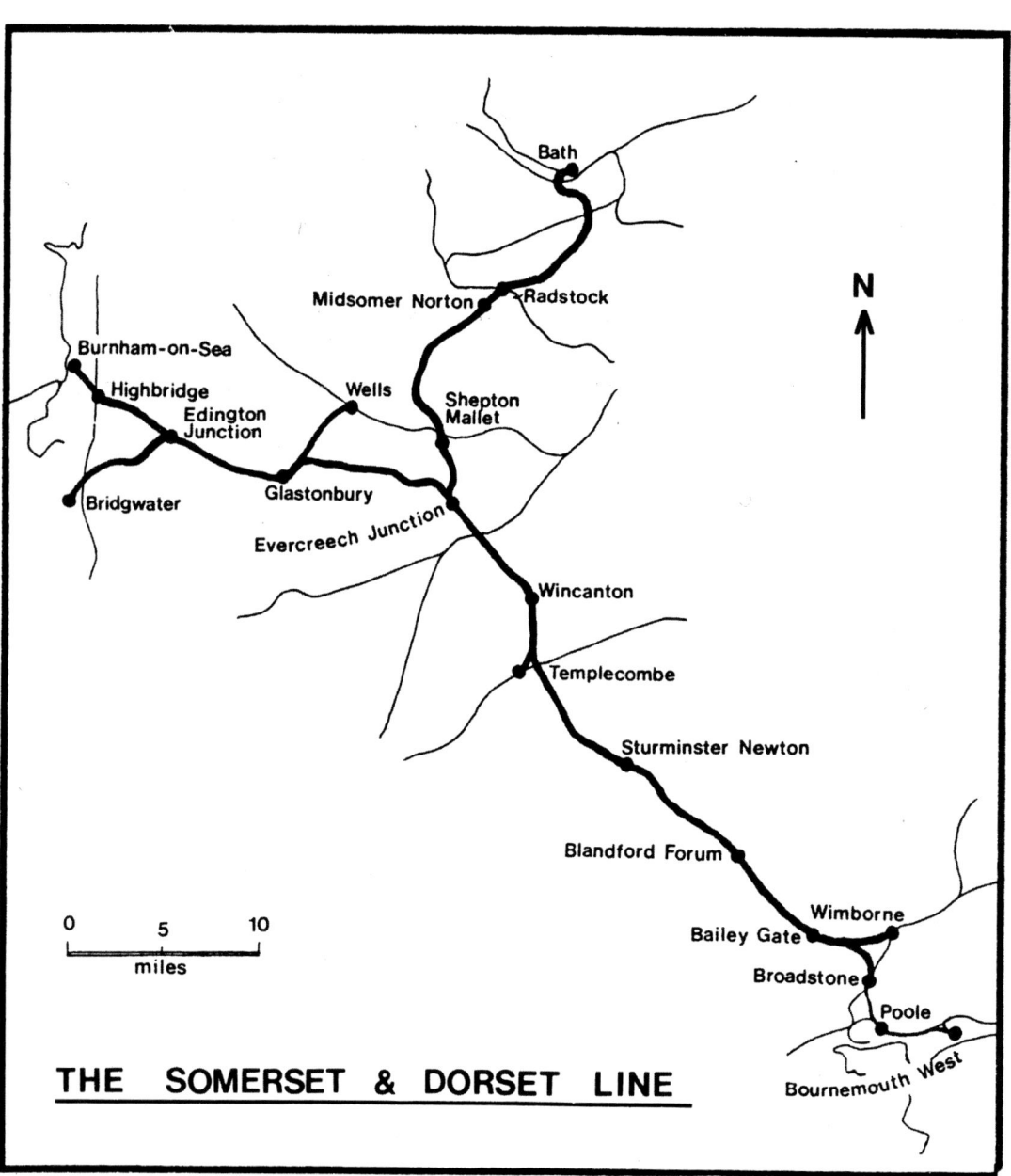

THE SOMERSET & DORSET LINE

Although not in direct competition with each other over most of their routes, the Big Four competed to be the fastest, most modern and most comfortable, spurred on by increasing competition from road transport. The financial motive of individual private companies was still the driving force behind the new, fewer companies.

Forced amalgamations – overcoming tensions and forging a new company

Not everyone was in favour of the creation of the Big Four. One prominent politician described it a an 'expensive and grandiose scheme, taken wantonly'. After the First World War ended, Parliament passed the Railways Act 1921 and so produced the Big Four railway companies emerging in 1923.

With a common focus, many rivalries can be put to one side and the greater good can prevail. However, when danger is averted, old animosities rise to the surface. Each of the new companies was formed from companies with different customers and different styles of operation. Thus, the LNER ran fast express trains up the East Coast of the country, whilst the Eastern Railway (ER) focused on mainly agricultural East Anglia with commuters into London, and the GCR had its domination of cross Pennine coal traffic. However, the latter company practically duplicated the MR routes in parts of Derbyshire, Yorkshire and Lancashire, and so its exclusion from an amalgamation with the ex-MR under the LMSR may have been a more practical approach. Illustrating the problem is the situation in Swinton, South Yorkshire. One road, aptly named Station Road, had three stations on it belonging to the MR, H&BR and Manchester, Sheffield and Lincolnshire Railway (MS&LR) companies. One of the first issues that the new Ministry of Transport examined was the condition of the country's signalling. Safety was paramount, especially in the public's eye, with over 11,000 signal boxes. Track circuiting, enabling signalmen to detect trains so they didn't get 'lost' or forgotten, had been feasible since 1872 but it was not mandatory for decades to come, instead relying on a signalman visually seeing a train.

The Big Four

This exemption from intense competition within the boardroom that handicapped other companies enabled the Southern Railway (SR) to concentrate on its core business. Moving large numbers of people was the company's main role. While the population in the country as a whole increased (by 10 per cent) the Home Counties, (and the SR's customers), grew by 13 per cent during the period 1923–37. In fact, the industrial north, Leeds, Sheffield and Manchester, experienced a decrease in population (1–2 per cent).

The task of producing a unified business from these three, as well as several other smaller companies, was a formidable task. However, it was made comparatively easier than the task facing the LMSR and the LNER as the SR was not involved in destructive infighting and its fortunes were dependent on varied industries. Of the twenty-one directors, it was not dominated by ones from any of the constituting railways. Appointing one skilled manager for well over a decade who was versed in government, business and academic spheres led to the interests of the shareholders and the railway commuters being reconciled.

Alternative Arrangements

The resultant 'Big Four' was not the only plan that was discussed. Others that were rejected included having Scotland as a railway company in its own right. However, with little traffic originating in that area, it was thought that this plan was unviable in the longer term. There was also a suggestion of combining the Midland and the Great Central railways as a rival to the LNWR was another possibility. The panel thought that the MR would cherry pick and dismantle the GCR resulting in an unviable situation. However, it would allow the MR access to east coast ports and the GCR better entry to Manchester.

The London, Midland and Scottish Railway (LMSR). This newly formed company was the result of the merger of some old, profitable and well-run companies. Which one of the three main partners was to run the new company? Was it to be from the old London and North Western Railway (LNWR), based at Crewe, the MR, located at Derby or the L&YR, emanating from Manchester? That is not forgetting the several other smaller companies who were also being merged, such as the North Staffordshire Railway (NSR), the Highland Railway (HR), the Caledonian Railway (CR), the Stratford-on-Avon Railway – later known as the Stratford-upon-Avon Railway (SAR) and the Maryport and Carlise Railway (M&CR). To bring out the best of these different companies would need a personality with vision and conviction. As it turned out, the influence of the MR won the day and their small engine policy prevailed. (BPC)

The Great Weatern Railway (GWR). This company had the fewest rivalries to contend with and so its future was very similar to the old business. This new company overpowered all of its constituents. In terms of mileage, the GWR covered the most miles, with 2,784 miles. Its nearest rival, the CR, boasted 244 miles, and Taff Vale Railway (TVR) only covered 112 miles. This clearly showed the GWR's dominant position. This illustrates the business of the GWR; exporting coal from the pits in South Wales and serving rural areas of central and northern Wales. The main business of the GWR was to transport passengers and goods from London to Bristol, the Midlands, South Wales and the West Country. It was not all plain sailing, though. The dominance of one partner can lead to complacency and reliance on traditional practices which may not be the best in an ever-changing business environment. (BPC)

The Southern Railway (SR). The company that, on paper, had an easier task, was those joining together to form the SR. However, the constituents majored in different fields; the London and South Western (LSWR), running express trains to the West Country, Plymouth and Southampton. The South Eastern and Chatham Railway (SE&CR) ran electrified commuter trains into London with extended trains to Dover. The London, Brighton and South Coast Railway (LB&SCR) ran both electrified commuter trains into London and extended trains from Portsmouth (LB&SCR)

The London and North Eastern Railway (LNER). Serving London, Newcastle and Edinburgh was the remit of the new LNER. This company, out of all of the Big Four was most dependent upon revenues from freight (60 per cent). This over reliance on one sector of operations was not called into question as future business seemed to be very similar of the present. It put under the same roof, the services of rural East Anglia, commuters of Essex, coal and steel industries of the North East, and expresses to York and Scotland – quite an eclectic set of undertakings. Only just finding its feet was the London extension of the GCR. The original segment of that railway – Manchester, Sheffield and Lincolnshire Railway (MS&LR) – was conveying vast quantities of coal for export via the deep-water port at Immingham and through the Woodhead tunnel through the Pennines to serve industries in Lancashire. Another coal carrying railway, the H&BR, had merged with the NER a year before the Grouping. (BPC)

CHAPTER 5
PERSONALITIES

In all of the newly formed companies, it was the appointment of forceful men with a clear vision and well able to navigate the boardroom compromises as well as argue forcefully the railways' perspective with the government of the day that was needed. They needed to galvanise their workforce to seize the opportunities that the new situation had produced.

Sir Eric Geddes. To many people he was the hero of the hour, advocating the formation of the Big Four against Conservative opposition in the forthcoming years, then cooperation rather than competition, would be able to take advantage of the new business arrangements. Steering a pathway was Minister of Transport Sir Eric Geddes, who was the first to hold this position in 1919. David Lloyd George once described him as 'a man of exceptional force and capacity'. However, he disliked the situation that he had to operate in and so resigned in 1921. There were five more appointments during that decade, and a further six throughout the following decade. This continual change at the top was the reason why many people believed that the country did not have a clear co-ordinated transport policy. No one was there long enough to have a 'grand plan' and to see it too fruition. Meanwhile, on the railwayman's side, a pamphlet from the Railway Clerks' Association (RCA) about the new regime promised its members that 'nationalisation will ensue'. This was in direct contrast to the creation of these four powerful companies who, it could be said, were trying to pre-empt, and indeed prevent, nationalisation. A battleground for the future.

Sir Hubert Walker. An insight into the rivalries between the men at the top can be gleaned by looking at what happened on the new Southern Region, an amalgamation of three companies. Initially, the board appointed not one but three general managers. Sir Hubert Walker was general manager of the LSWR from 1 January 1912 and by January 1917 he was the acting chairman of the REC for which he was made a Knight Commander of the Order of the Bath (KCB). The company opted for Walker, retiring the other two managers. He worked as the general manager until 1937 and served on the SR board until its demise in 1947, giving the company great stability. The SR's profitability in later years can, in part, be attributed to having stability at the top.

The other railway companies had similar issues, more general managers than were needed. In the LNER, one of the contenders was approaching retirement, another had been seduced to work in Canada and two others lacked ambition and almost by default Ralph Wedgewood took over as general manager.

If ever there were contrasts to be looked at it would be between the GWR and the LMSR. The GWR absorbed several smaller companies, the general managers of which were not candidates for the role of general manager of the new region, which Charles Benjamin Collett ascended to. However, the LMSR incorporated several large and successful companies so there were a number of general managers from which to make a selection.

Josiah Stamp. The LMSR was almost the complete opposite. Its lines made up over 60 per cent of the total for the country, it really was a very large company and incorporated three large companies (L&YR, LNWR and MR) as well as a number of medium sized enterprises. All this led to several candidates for the top job and diplomacy for dealing with potentially warring factions. Needless to say its inception was neither smooth nor rapid, both hampering its potential for success, at least four of the constituents were ex-rivals – hardly a recipe for success. It took until 1926 for some of the dust to settle on Josiah Stamp. As the chairman and he was instrumental in getting William Stanier appointed as chief mechanical engineer (CME) in 1932 (from the GWR) to solve the company's locomotive problems. Stamp served until 1941.

CHAPTER 6
THE EARLY YEARS

No sooner had the dust settled on the Grouping in 1923, the next year the country was to hold an exhibition at Wembley, in North London. The idea for this exhibition had been circulating since 1902 but it only really took off from 1920. As well as a stadium with a football field and running track inside, exhibitors came from all over the globe. In some ways it signified the end of the British Empire and heralded new world powers like the USA and Russia in

British Empire Exhibition, 1924. The idea was that each part of the British Empire should have an area of land to showcase their country. This is an aerial view of the exhibition site giving some idea of the scale. A purpose-built 'great national sports ground', called the Empire Stadium, was built for the exhibition. It could hold 125,000 people, 30,000 of them seated. Although it incorporated a football pitch, it was not solely intended as a football stadium. Its quarter mile running track, incorporating a 220-yard straight track (the longest in the country) was seen as being at least equally important. The only standard gauge locomotive involved in the construction of the stadium has survived, and still runs on the late Sir William McAlpine's private Fawley Hill Railway near Henley-on-Thames, which is well worth a visit. (BPC)

economic and naval power. It was officially opened by George V on 23 April 1923 – St George's Day and William Shakespeare's birthday, a truly British event. Nearby stations on the national network were re-vamped to cope with the expected crowds. Wembley Park station (Metropolitan line) at the north of the site was re-built as was Wembley Hill (ex-GCR) at the south. However, recognising that these stations alone could not cope with the number of visitors and with an eye on its use as the national stadium for future sporting and other events, a new station was built in the exhibition grounds itself.

Railway exhibits

All of the Big Four railway companies had display stands exhibiting their latest locomotives or coaches including the locomotives below.

No. 4472 *Flying Scotsman* (LNER) and No. 4079 *Pendennis Castle* (GWR). While the latter won the technical battle of 'most powerful passenger engine in Gt. Britain', the former won the publicity battle. The LMSR managed a black painted Prince of Wales Class 4-6-0 locomotive and the SR displayed posters of beauty spots they served. The next year the SR managed to exhibit an N Class engine, which was brand new, not entering service until 28 November 1925. (BPC)

Stockton and Darlington (S&DR) Centenary, 1925

Even before the dust had time to settle on the future organisation of the country's railways it was time for an exhibition to celebrate in great style the centenary of the opening of the S&DR. This celebration of railways was planned at the locomotive works of the SD&R in Faverdale. Scheduled for June 1925 (the actual centenary would be in the September) it was attended by royalty and consisted of a cavalcade of engines depicting progress over the last 100 years. This aerial view is of the site where the celebrations were held. To celebrate 100 years of railways since the opening of the S&DR the LNER put on a centenary exhibition in Faverdale, Darlington, between Dinsdale and Eaglescliffe stations. A special grandstand was built so that locomotives could parade in front of distinguished guests including HRH the Duke of York on 1 July. In typical early railway tradition, after the opening ceremony and parade, the 700 guests adjourned to a banquet held in the adjacent wagon works' paint shop.

There was a good reason for holding the centenary celebrations in July. The International Railway Congress, consisting of representatives of the railways of the world, meets every five years. This year the congregation was due to meet in Spain, but in view of the celebration of a century of British railway, their committee suggested

Exhibits. A locomotive from Hetton Colliery Lyon led the parade. After the procession, visitors were welcome to visit to the Faverdale Works of the LNER, where a great collection of railway relics was on exhibition. Here were objects that would delight the heart of every reader – pictures and prints, documents and books regarding the early railways; early forms of signalling apparatus; permanent way materials – early railway lines, points, stone sleepers, etc., models of locomotives; early railway carriages, and hundreds of other things of equal interest. On the sidings outside the exhibition buildings were the locomotives and rolling stock that had taken part in the morning's procession. The celebrations were opened on Thursday, 2 July 1925 by the Duke and Duchess of York. After the centenary celebrations, the question arose, 'What to do with these old artifacts?' One consequence of these celebrations was the production of a list of seventy-one engines for preservation and the establishment of a railway museum in York. (BPC)

The LNER Garrett. The exhibits ranged from (replicas of) locomotives that hauled coal wagons 100 years ago to those currently working and about to start work, what a contrast. One exhibit in this latter category was, the LNER Garrett, described as, 'the most powerful locomotive in the world'. This is exhibit No. 42 on the parade. It was actually two freight locomotive power units with a single massive boiler slung between the two. There were discussions when the locomotive was at the design stage for there to be two such engines, but in the end, only one was built, by Beyer, Peacock and Company at their East Manchester Works, which was the opposite side of the tracks to the ex-GCR works at Gorton. (RAS)

that if the meeting could be held in July, instead of on the actual date of the anniversary in September, they would hold their 1925 session in London instead of in Madrid. Delegates travelled to Darlington, where the centenary of the railway was celebrated on the site of the original S&DR.

Locomotive trials 1925, also known as, 'The Great Exchange'

At the exhibition in 1924, the GWR declared their smaller engine to be more powerful than its rival, the LNER. GWR's general manager goaded the LNER southern area general manager that a trial of the two types should take place via an exchange arrangement. The LNER officials were quietly confident that the lighter, smaller GWR engine would be unable to haul their typical 480-ton train up Holloway Bank on the exit from King's Cross and so eagerly awaited the start. However, the GWR locomotive made a faster start from King's Cross than any of their own engines had recorded up to that time, and over the trial *Pendennis Castle* kept well within the scheduled time. It also used less coal, considerably denting LNER's pride.

36 • THE RAILWAY GROUPING 1923 TO THE BEECHING ERA

GWR representative. The resulting trials commenced in April 1925 with No. 4079 *Pendennis Castle* representing the GWR on the GNR main line. (BPC)

The LNER delegate. No. 4474 *Victor Wild* representing the LNER on Great Western tracks, although seen here passing Newton on a revenue earning train from Manchester to Sheffield. The Cornish Rivera Express was the chosen service for comparisons. Although *Victor Wild* kept to time, the longer wheelbase of the LNER Pacific proved unsuited to the many curves on the route. The GWR took the honours, using a different engine of the same class, with *Caldicot Castle* burning less fuel and always ahead of time, this being illustrated on the last two days of the trial by gaining fifteen minutes on the schedule in both directions. (BPC)

Dynameter car. Apart from actual trials there were two other methods of assessing an engine's performance. One was to tow a special carriage that measures different aspects of the performance, a dynameter car. This is the one belonging to the GWR. (Photomatic)

Testing table. The other method was to use a static testing table. This one, at Swindon, dates from 1905, the other was at Rugby. It allowed an engine to perform as if it was on the track, allowing measurements to be made. To see and hear an engine, such as the one illustrated below, being driven at over 50mph while stationary must have been an awesome sight. Engine No. 2931 *Arlington Grange* is on the testing table. (BPC)

38 • THE RAILWAY GROUPING 1923 TO THE BEECHING ERA

Other Trials

Another trial, over the LMSR lines between London and Carlisle, in 1926, involving a Castle Class engine (No. 5000 *Launceston Castle*) showed its superiority, so much so that the LMSR directors requested that the GWR build a class of such engines for use on their West Coast Main Line. This was rejected by the GWR board of directors. Subsequently, a full set of construction drawings was requested. As the two companies were not in direct competition, it is hard to understand why the GWR directors refused this also.

Locomotive visit 1927. The year marked the centenary of the Baltimore and Ohio Railroad, the first common carrier railroad in the USA, and they wanted to celebrate this by holding the Fair of the Iron Horse to be held near Baltimore, Maryland. The organisers hoped that a British locomotive could be included. Hot on the heels of the comparative tests, in reality this meant a GWR Castle Class locomotive. However, intervention by Sir Felix Pole, the chairman of the GWR, meant that one of the latest engines was to be made ready. After close examination of a suitable name, and re-naming several Star Class engines, No. 6000 *King George V* was completed and tested on runs on the line to Plymouth in July 1927. A Westinghouse vacuum pump had to be fitted, spoiling the sleek lines, on the right-hand side to comply with American methods of braking. That month the engine, the pride of the GWR, was exhibited in Paddington station and went on a tour of its territory where it was enthusiastically greeted by crowds of people. (BPC)

Voyage across 'The Pond'. To ship the locomotive from Cardiff docks as deck cargo, it had to be dismantled and cradled in timbers, for the (mostly, uneventful) journey to the USA. Here the boiler is being lifted out from the frame, prior to both being lifted onto its carriage, *Chicago City* across 'The Pond'. William Stanier, later of LMSR fame, accompanied the group of GWR personnel to the USA. In typical American style, its arrival was greeted by enthusiastic crowds, before and during the procession at the celebrations (as number 28), much like those at Stockton earlier passed dignitaries. On returning to England, it continued to earn its keep as a haulier of express trains. With their Royal Scot engines rolling off the production lines at Crewe, the LMSR were less than pleased by all the publicity given to *King George V*, however, the supremacy of the King Class was acknowledged by all. (BPC)

CHAPTER 7
THE ECONOMIC CONDITIONS AFTER THE GROUPING

The amalgamation of railway companies to form the Big Four was probably the action that saved many of them from going bankrupt. Although the general outlook was pessimistic; profitable lines carried the weaker ones. As long as an overall profit was made then cross subsiding was accepted. As private companies, the Big Four were able to pay reasonable dividends to their shareholders immediately following their formation. This, in part, was due to the problems on

Mounted police face striking miners, Sheffield. There were two miners' strikes in the decade, the one in 1926 leading to the General Strike. Coal mining was a very emotive business. Just after the First World War it employed 1.25 million, mostly men. Faced with falling demand, the mine owners believed that the route to prosperity lay with wage reductions, longer hours and colliery closures. Needless to say their attitude led to disputes with the miners. Stoppage of work in the coalfields in 1926 soon led to an exhaustion of coal stocks including reserves. This led to the importation of coal from the USA, the mine owners bearing the brunt of this extra cost. Britain's world trade fell by half between 1929 and 1933, the output of heavy industry fell by a third, employment profits plunged in nearly all sectors. The continued tight monetary and fiscal policies led to a four-year long recession, known as the 'The Slump'. The Bank of England raised the base rate to 7 per cent and the monetary policy focused on the return to the 'gold standard'. At the depth in the summer of 1932, the registered unemployed numbered 3.5 million, and many more had only part-time employment. (BPC)

mainland Europe caused by the First World War and the occupation of the Rhine-Ruhr industrial complex. The terms of the peace agreement following the war meant that massive reparations were to be paid to the French by the German government. The payments were defaulted upon so much that the French sent in troops in January 1923 to occupy the industrial base of the German economy. The Ruhr occupation, as it became known, would last more than two and a half years and it had a profound effect on both politics and the economy of the Weimar Republic. Unable to produce goods and with workers to pay, the German national treasury was very nearly empty and cash reserves were insufficient for paying 2 million striking industrial workers. The government's last resort was to pay these salaries by ordering the printing of extra banknotes. This policy contributed to the rampant hyperinflation of 1923 in Germany. Many objects became more valuable than money. A wheelbarrow would be worth more than all the highest denomination banknotes it could carry. It needs to be remembered that things were not entirely rosy at home, with unemployment peaking at 9 per cent, hampering the country by its reliance on old, staple industries for exports just as other countries were starting to develop their own after the conflict.

Jarrow March, 1936. What started out as a protest of men made unemployed due to the hardened attitudes of the mine owners, led to a walk from Jarrow, on Tyneside, to London. Everywhere they went, more people joined in. They did reach their destination and handed in their petition but achieved little else except a place in the folk lore of the country. The (main) cause was a coal strike that began many years earlier on 31 March 1921 with coal rationing introduced on 3 April 1921. The strike ended on 28 June 1921 and helps explain the sharp recovery in July of that year. The miners' strike contributed to the loss of some 85.9 million working days in 1921, which was just over a half of the 162.2 million days lost during the better-known General Strike of 1926.

General Strike, 1926

The strike lasted from 3–12 May in 1926. It was called by the Trades Union Congress from one minute to midnight on 3 May 1926. For the previous two days, some 1 million coal miners had been locked out of their mines after a dispute with the owners who wanted them to work longer hours for less money. In solidarity, huge numbers from other industries stayed off work, including bus, rail and dock workers, as well as people with printing, gas, electricity, building, iron, steel and chemical jobs. The aim was to force the government to act to prevent mine owners reducing miners' wages by 13 per cent and increasing their shifts from seven to eight hours. The industrial action came against a backdrop of tough economic times following the First World War and a growing fear of communism. Heavy industries which formed the bedrock of Britain's export trade (such as coal mining, shipbuilding and steel) were heavily concentrated in certain areas of Britain, such as northern England, South Wales, Northern Ireland and central Scotland, whilst the newer industries were heavily concentrated in southern and central England. British industrial output during the 1920s ran at about 80–100 per cent, and exports at about 80 per cent of their pre-war levels. Between the Grouping and almost the start of hostilities in 1938 passenger numbers dropped by 30 per cent, freight by 9 per cent and coal by 14 per cent. The printing presses ground to a virtual halt and food deliveries were held up.

'**Helpers**'. This is a group of Oxford University students, 'helping' in the strike; there were several such instances. One comment suggests that no matter how well intended the volunteers were, they were just that, volunteers. For the Ministry of Transport to allow, or encourage, such actions must be seen as bordering on criminal negligence; luckily disaster never occurred. A group of volunteers are helping, or hindering, the paralysis on the railways. The transport network was crippled without its bus and train drivers, and roads became choked with cars. Over the nine days that the strike lasted there were clashes between strikers and police in London, Liverpool and Hull. The government reacted by trying to take control of the media and published its own propaganda newspaper *The British Gazette*, which was highly patriotic and critical of the strikers. The TUC then decided to print its own newspaper – *The British Worker*, but circulation for *The British Gazette* was much greater. Nine days after it began, the TUC called off the strike, following secret discussions with the mine owners. The miners had won no concessions for their cause. The strikers slowly returned to work apart from the miners who struggled on until November 1926, eventually having to return to work with less money and more hours. (BPC)

CHAPTER 8
RAILWAY FINANCES

The development and modernisation of railway transport

Following the economic conditions of the 1920s, the country was in a dilemma. It did not own the Big Four railway companies but could not function without them. The plan was to encourage them to perform the role that they had shown was essential in the First World War to try and reduce unemployment. Two significant pieces of legislation were passed by Parliament in 1929, 'Passenger Duty Works' and 'Development (Loans, Guarantees & Grants Act'. The former was designed to assist railways in new works while the latter was a scheme of work for the relief of unemployment.

Trying to attribute new works to each Act is almost impossible, partially due to the time taken to perform the work with delays attributing a work incorrectly to a different Act. For clarity, the works have been gathered together under the umbrella of 1930s improvements, on a regional basis, by type of work.

Paddington station. The GWR tried to improve Isambard Kingdom Brunel's 'Billiard table' line to Bristol. Following a report in the late 1920s, the company embarked on an ambitious scheme to re-model its affairs at Paddington station early in the 1930s. Platforms at their London terminus were elongated, and concrete replaced wood. Heading west, Didcot Junction station was re-modelled and two extra lines were built at Challow and Uffington stations. This enabled faster trains to overtake slower, stopping freight trains. (BPC)

Great Western Railway (GWR) Avoiding Lines

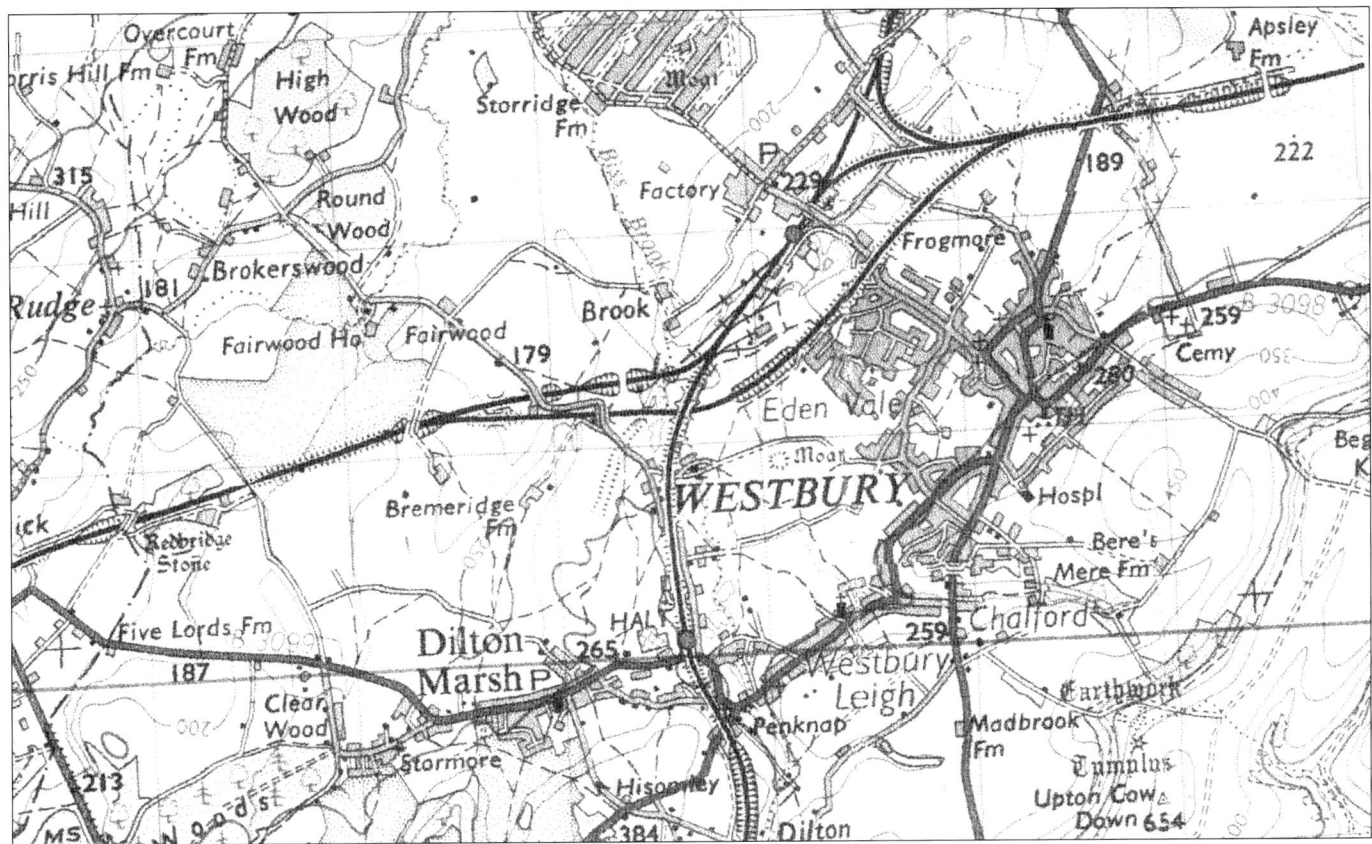

Improving the 'Great Way Round': Westbury and Frome avoiding lines

The GWR was often referred to as the 'Great Way Round', and the injection of money into the GWR was seized upon as a way of speeding up its traffic to Exeter. Until that time, the Great Way Round' had been via Bristol, hence the sobriquet. It was the construction of lines around Castle Cary to the existing Bristol to Exeter line at Cogload Junction in 1906 in an attempt to get London trains to the West Country quicker than the 'Great Way Round' that led to the transformation of Frome from a station on a secondary north to south line, to one on a main east to west route. When the cut-off line from Reading to Taunton via Westbury was opened, it ran through Westbury and Frome stations. Westbury was not originally aligned for an east-west main line, and Frome station was on an awkward curve; there was a 30mph speed restriction at both places for the west of England and Weymouth trains, and at Westbury they conflicted with the heavy coal traffic from the Trowbridge line towards Salisbury. Using the money from the government, the company built avoiding lines bypassing each station. Logan and Hemingway of Doncaster was the contractor, and the cost of the works was to be £220,000. The avoiding lines were opened to goods traffic on 1 January 1933, and for all traffic at the beginning of the summer timetable in 1933. As you leave Westbury station on a train for Salisbury, you pass over the avoiding line.

In 1933, a connection from the Stert line ran along a new route to the east of Westbury station and re-joined the main line some distance to the west. Another connection was opened in 1942 to allow westbound trains from the Stert line to run directly to the north towards Chippenham or Bristol, one of many short connecting

Westbury map. This map shows the 2.25 mile long avoiding Westbury line between Heywood Road Junction (nearer London) and Fairwood Junction, which was opened in 1933.

lines built around the network during the Second World War. In 1933, a Frome bypass route was constructed, enabling through traffic to avoid the station and the junction with the Radstock branch, and leaving the station on a looped branch as at present. (BPC)

Taunton

In the 1930s the lines through Taunton from Cogload Junction to Norton Fitzwarren were widened from two to four tracks; those east of Taunton were brought into use on 13 December 1931 and those to the west on 14 February 1932. This work forced another rebuilding of the station. The train shed was dismantled, and new buildings constructed on the up (north) side along with a new island platform in the middle of the station. This gave a platform face for each of the four through lines, which were brought into use on 7 February 1932. Work included a new subway that replaced the old footbridge.

Taunton entrance. This rebuild involved a new booking office at road level on the north side of the station, albeit on a smaller scale than Leamington. The exterior had stonework faced with white Portland stone, one corporate style that persisted though. The company name is written in large letters into the facing stone and the station's name is on the meagre canopy. The old goods shed was replaced by a two-storey goods warehouse next to the avoiding line, east of the station on 20 February 1932.

Westbury, date unknown. One of the trains the bypass was intended for was the Up Cornish Rivera Express. Here, on the bypass is the celebrated engine No. 6000 *King George V* on its way to London. Besides name-boards on the coaches, the first three vehicles are of the centenary stock variety with their recessed doors and slightly wider body. Two sets of thirteen centenary coaches were built in 1935 to celebrate 100 years of the GWR and they entered service on the Cornish Riviera Limited trains with the summer timetable on 8 July of that year. They were built to a similar design as the super saloons with 9ft 7in width bodies, which restricted the route availability, and until the outbreak of the Second World War only worked the Cornish Riviera. The width of the vehicle maximises comfort inside but necessitated recessing of the doors. The centenary special edition of the *GWR Magazine* notes, in a review of how passenger comfort has improved over the previous 100 years, commented:

> To celebrate the Company's centenary two new corridor trains have been constructed at Swindon and put into service on the 'Cornish Riviera Limited Expresses'. They mark a distinct departure from previous practice as the vehicles are fitted with two end doors only on each side, with spacious vestibules. This has enabled large drop windows to be fitted to each compartment. Spring fitted cushions and fluted seat backs enhance the seats and make the contrast with the conditions of third class travel of even much less than a century ago, well-nigh unbelievable.

After the Second World War, the centenary coaches were no longer restricted to the 'Limited' but could be seen on most main line services including Newbury race specials.

The Wombourne branch

Wombourne station. The Wolverhampton and Kingswinford Railway (W&KR) was seen as a link to Wolverhampton, and it was necessary to reduce congestion around Wolverhampton and its line to Shrewsbury. Originating north of Brettell Lane station, it re-connected north of Wolverhampton Low Level station with a triangular junction at Oxley, adjacent to the engine shed. Construction of the new line began in 1913, but work was halted within three years following the outbreak of the First World War. After the war ended in 1918, construction resumed. The GWR Additional Powers Act 1924, which sought to extend the date for opening to 1925 also renewed the authorisation for the postponed Bridgnorth extension. The Wombourne branch opened for passenger traffic in May 1925, but passenger numbers proved disappointing, and services were discontinued in 1932 after just seven years. The Bridgnorth extension was never completed. This is one of the main stations at Wombourne, others were at Tettenhall and Himley with a number of smaller halts. Freight traffic used it to avoid Wolverhampton station. (BPC)

London, Midland and Scottish Railway (LMSR) New Lines

Milford signal box. Money was also used to relieve a short (1½ mile) section of line north of Duffield in Derbyshire. This was acting as a bottleneck on the ex-MR line to Derby and Manchester. Short as the distance may be, complex was the order of the day with two viaduct river crossings and a deep cutting at Longland. The building was started in May 1930. This is the small signal box which controlled the joining of the lines before they enter the tunnel. The signals are to direct Derby-bound trains along the main or goods line. (BPC)

Mirfield

The L&YR's Calder Valley line was a vital artery when coal was king, so much so that it progressively quadrupled from around 1900. However, in Mirfield, South Yorkshire, the line passes over the River Calder. The Up/Down tracks part company for the creation of a long, wide island platform for the station. The original stone bridge taking two lines over the water became a serious bottleneck to the smooth running of the line. In 1932, two extra lines were laid across the river and to the south of Mirfield station, in all ¾ of a mile.

Mirfield station. This more modern view is from almost the ends of Mirfield station platform, looking west. Hurrying east with a load of empty mineral wagons the Austerity engine No. 90642. It is travelling along the new down fast line while the original pair of lines serve the island platform. The opportunity was taken by the LMSR to experiment with speed signalling here. Mirfield is on the ex-L&YR main line and was heavily used by Leeds to Manchester (ex-LNWR) trains, around 2.75 miles between Thornhill and Heaton Lodge junctions. Here, a little further towards Heaton Lodge Junction, is yet another east bound empty mineral train behind Stanier engine No. 48771. The short section of the ex-L&YR line that they shared with the ex-LNWR was the subject of an interesting signalling experiment. As can be seen, semaphore signals have been replaced by colour lights in an attempt to control trains' speed. (R.K. Blencowe)

Deal Street, Manchester. In an attempt to mitigate against, 'considerable difficulty in dealing with heavy traffic at Victoria and Exchange station[s] due to a lack of platform space' (LMSR Traffic Committee, 29 March 1923), the company planned 'No. 11 platform at Victoria be extended to the west end of Exchange No 3 platform and additional running road from which trains could be into either of three sections of the new platform'. Incidentally, at 2,238ft this new platform became the longest in the world when opened in April 1929. Extensive new crossovers and re-modelling enabled both stations to serve destinations normally the preserve of one of them. A complete re-signalling scheme was undertaken by Westinghouse for a contract price of £64,892. This involved the replacement of the No. 2 boxes at Deal Street (L&YR), and Exchange and Salford stations (LNWR), and Deal Street also received a new power box with ninety-nine levers between the ex-L&YR and ex-LNER lines. (BPC)

London and North Eastern Railway (LNER) new lines

***Above and below*: Ilford.** In 1931/32 the LNER quadrupled the tracks to Shenfield, which became the terminus for inner-suburban operation. On the ex-GER lines out of Liverpool Street there was call to electrify the line as far as Shenfield (en route to Colchester), exchanges between the lines could take place at Stratford. This called for major engineering works including widening of the lines and a flyover at Ilford. To cope with demand, the former GER line to Ongar was developed as an extension of the Central Line of the Underground system.

Work on the scheme to electrify the line between Liverpool Street and Shenfield was well under way before the outbreak of the Second World War in 1939. A major project was the construction of a flyover on the site of Aldersbrook sidings, west of Ilford. This enabled electric trains access to the new depot on the north side of the line between Ilford and Manor Park. A local train is using the flyover and a long distance train is at ground level. The £7.5 million scheme would reduce conflict and lead to a speeding up of local services and less delays to main line traffic.

Many years later, when the wires at Ilford were energised, to assist in moving units around the sidings, a redundant banking engine was utilised. (Both BPC)

Tollerton. Further south, almost at the halfway point between London and Edinburgh, is Tollerton station. Here, the old station buildings were swept away, with slow lines either side of the fast lines. To allow passenger access, new platforms and facilities were built to serve the slow lines. At Thirsk, a different plan was adopted with two island platforms being created. (BPC)

Works on the East Coast Main Line

Northallerton

This town is a crossroad of two very important routes. From Newcastle in the north is the East Coast Main Line heading south to York. Creating junctions are the lines from Middlesbrough and Teesside in the east and Ripon to the west. To increase capacity south from here the company allocated over £250,000 of improvement monies to rebuild the line to York, the programme having been started many years earlier in 1897. As this line carried all the company's freight from Tyneside, Teesside and Scotland to the south as well as heavy and important passenger traffic, it was a vital artery. Bridges were replaced and the quadrupling of the lines took different forms.

London and North Eastern Railway (LNER) Stations

Welwyn Garden City. When a new 'Garden City' was planned in Hertfordshire, it eventually took the name of its adjacent town, Welwyn. To accommodate the station, the outer lines of the quadruple tracks of the East Coast Main Line, were eased out so that two island platforms could be squeezed in. This led to issues over passenger access. The main station buildings were remote from the lines and connected to them by a long footbridge. At opening in 1926, the buildings off to the right, with the covered footbridge, joined the buildings on the two island platforms. This led to a situation that was unsafe as passengers from the east could access the island platform by trespassing on railway land with its inherent dangers. Later, in 1935, the left-hand end of the footbridge was extended over the goods yard and connected to the roads, and the now listed building, in which the Shredded Wheat factory is located. An additional booking office was also opened at that time. The opening on the clean clear lines, with four lines and additional platform lines would encourage fast-running trains. (BPC)

Southern Railway (SR) Stations

Stations rebuilt in 1930s

Canon Street station, London. Hailed as one of the greatest engineering feats of modern times, the LR and SE&CR had services terminating in London at Holborn Viaduct, Charing Cross and Canon Street. Lines from all three met at Borough Market Junction, just north of London Bridge station, but south of the River Thames. By the start of the 1920s, the whole system was beginning to creak and lacked capacity. When Continental boat trains from Charing Cross were originated, they only added to the difficulties that the suburban traffic encountered. In order to solve the issues, the SR took the bold step of closing down the junction between 5 and 28 June 1926. The station was closed to allow them to carry out various works, including the rebuilding of the platforms, relaying of the tracks and installation of a new system of electrical signalling – the four-aspect colour light scheme. The station was also renovated, and the glass roof cleaned. The number of platforms was reduced from nine to eight, with five set aside for the new electric trains. The signal box spanning the width of the railway bridge was removed. Illustrating the complexity of the work, this picture shows the lines being ripped out and new ones being inserted. The sheer number of men, cranes and materials necessitated a careful watch be kept on safety.

Chessington Branch

Branching south-west from the Mole Valley line at Motspur Park, this short line was destined for Leatherhead. However, it was only built as far as Chessington South. Along the way are stations at Tolworth and Chessington South.

Malden Manor. This concrete method of construction was in keeping with the Art Deco style of its time. This was the last line, electrified at opening, built by the Southern Region. It was opened in stages, to serve Malden Manor and Tolworth (29 May 1938) and a year later serving Chessington (North and South). They were named Chessington Court and Chessington Grange respectively. The housing and light engineering projections for the land from Surbiton to Leatherhead did not materialise. Different ideas after the Second World War produced the concept of a 'Green Belt' around cities and the projected extension of the line fell foul of such ideas and was consequently never built.

Works that the public did not see

All the Big Four companies used the money for works that often the public were unaware of but that assisted in their efficiency. This assisted in the smooth flow of goods, and servicing engines. This section deals with the new works at March, which was typical of what was going on all over the country.

Steam engines needed to be stored somewhere when not being used. Most common were straight sheds with multiple roads although some companies adopted a roundhouse approach. For some reason, in the 1930s programme, new/rebuilt sheds were of five-road design. One thing engines did was to emit sulphurous exhaust gases. These, being damp, were mildly acidic and so the roofs of sheds corroded and needed replacing. There was another method to prevent corrosion. This involved coating the supports in reinforced concrete. This was tried at Frodingham when it was built in 1931.

Left: **March coaling tower.** Unseen by the public, replenishing an engine's coal store is not a simple matter. To put more than 5 tons of coal into a tender, quickly, needs special buildings in appropriate places. The traditional method was for men to shovel coal from a wagon into a tub and then push the tub next to the tender and then to upend it so filling the tender. This needed a special building and a number of men to perform the task and there was always another engine coming along behind needing coaling. The new schemes involved building a tall concrete tower and hoisting the coal wagons up into the air. The wagon would tip its contents into a bunker containing in excess of 60 tons of coal. In this system, several engines could be refuelled rapidly and fewer men were needed. These tall buildings were obvious beacons for enemy aircraft during any future conflict. This was not foremost in the designers' minds and thankfully, nor in the bombers' either.

Below: **March engine shed.** With the rise of the adjacent Whitemoor marshalling yard and the general growth in business, March shed was unable to cope. In the early 1930s, the LNER built a new locomotive shed with a mechanical coaling plant. Using local materials, a brick built five-track straight through washout shed was added in 1933. A water softener with a capacity of 11,700 gallons per hour was added in 1939, at a cost of over £12,000. (J. Suter)

New marshalling yards, March.
(All pictures *BPC* except 858 *R.K. Blencowe Negative Archive*)

To handle the agricultural products and general freight between East Anglia, London and the Midlands as well as coal from the East Midlands and northern England there were several old yards at their cross roads near March in Cambridgeshire. As engines became more powerful, trains became longer and the old sidings in March simply could not cope. Wagons waiting to be sorted had to be held as far away as Peterborough. There were just 24 sidings in the old yard with a capacity of 1,265, far short of the demand.

The 'hump'. The whole train was then pushed over a specially made 'hump' of track some 13–15ft high. Labelled as, 'Whitemoor a focal point between East England and the North', with finances now available, the LNER took the opportunity to replace the old yards with new marshalling yards, the up yard completed in 1929 and the down yard in 1933. Upon arrival in the reception sidings, the train of wagons are uncoupled according to their destination and a 'cut' card being made up and sent to the controlling tower. Controlling events is the small building on the right.

WHITEMOOR YARD
VIEW OF RIGHT HAND SIDE OF

Hump engine. This photograph is of the S Class 0-8-4T at Wath, South Yorkshire (another hump yard) prior to it being sent to Whitemoor (March) in 1933. Note the worker on the right with the pole to enable him to separate the wagons, connected by a three link coupling. Gravity now pulled the wagons into the sorting sidings, the points having been pre-set by the control tower according to the cut card. There were rail brakes that gripped the wheels' flange, slowing them down and thereby avoiding the collisions that other yards experienced. At its peak, the up yard dealt with 145 loaded trains each day. Engines were then attached to the wagons in the sidings and the train left the yard. When diesel shunters were in their infancy they were trialled here. So important was Whitemoor yard to the country's Second World War effort that a decoy yard was built 4 miles away to distract the enemy's bombers; attempts to verify this and for photographic evidence have proved fruitless.

New marshalling yard at Banbury (GWR). A new hump yard opened in 1931 at Banbury. Ever since the connection from here to the GCR opened in 1900, traffic had increased. After years of slowly increasing the number of blind ending sidings, in 1930 the company converted them into loops. At their northern end, after four reception lines, was an elevated section of track – 'the hump' – leading to eighteen loops into which wagons could be sorted. At their southern end, the loops combined and led to the east of the station, eventually connecting to the main lines. Off to the left is North Junction signal box with the main line further to the left. On the right are the ends of the sorting sidings with their compliment of wagons. Two engines await their next duty, and two engines are assembling their loads. On the right, No. 2816 is getting ready to take the 9.00 am to Old Oak Common while on the left is the Hall Class No. 5982 *Harrington Hall*. Its train will be taken to Westbury. On the extreme left are some guard's vans on a raised incline. To attach one of these wagons to a train, it would pull forward and the guard would slowly release the brake on the wagons which, if done with due care and attention, would slowly trundle down the incline and lie next to the last wagon. After coupling up and various whistles and flag waving, the train driver would set off under the bridge and bypass Banbury station on his way south. The hump yard had 19 sidings and was capable of holding 1,400 wagons. (BPC)

Dock Works

The LNER was the largest dock owner of the Big Four and relied upon its docks for a sizeable proportion of its income.

Parkston Quay West. A station, also known as Harwich, opened for steamer services only from 1 October 1934. This was in response to overcrowding as the company was a victim of its own success. The company's 'night parade' was of three ships sailing within a few minutes of each other; the 10.00 pm for the Hook of Holland, Antwerp and Zeebruge, which forced them to enlarge the docks. Trains would arrive to the platform. Passengers would disembark and walk through the shed to their waiting ship, at the jetty on the right. (BPC)

CHAPTER 9
ELECTRIFICATION SCHEMES

Most of the railway companies inherited different electrified systems, some with overhead wires and some third rail. The GWR's amalgamated companies (at least one or more) had not developed electrification to move passengers.

With four different systems and different voltages, the industry welcomed a government committee to look at the issue of electrification at the same time as the Railways Act was being debated. The Electricity (Supply) Act 1926 laid the foundations of our present-day national grid unifying the current over 600 different companies supplying electricity – alternating current (AC) and direct current (DC) – at varying voltages. After the legislation came into effect, companies had to supply an electrical alternating current at 50 cycles per second. This meant that the railway companies were able to tap into local supplies rather than each one having to build their own supply system. However, it took until 1927 and a committee chaired by Lord Pringle (Chief Inspector of Railways) to recommend the next year that there be two standard voltages, both direct current, overhead at 1,500V and third rail at 750V, excluding underground lines. The later Weir Committee, in 1929, looked at main line electrification but none of the Big Four were contemplating long distance electrification.

Apart from the ex-MR scheme at Lancashire and Morcambe and the SR 'Overhead Electric Railway' in south London – which had overhead wires – most schemes used the three rail contact principle. Those that did build them concentrated chiefly in large towns and cities, usually in response to the competition from electric trams running along the roads. Hence the LMSR inherited schemes from the L&YR around Manchester to Bury as well as the Liverpool schemes to Southport, Ormskirk and Kirkby. There were two schemes, under the River Mersey to Birkenhead and sections of the ex-Wirral Railway (WR) to West Kirkby and New Brighton. The LNER also had more than one system: live rail (third) in Newcastle and overhead out of Liverpool Street in London.

Southern Railway (SR)

The LB&SCR line from Victoria had been electrified (pre-Grouping) as far as Three Bridges, now it was to be extended to Brighton, the company using the money to continue their electrification to Brighton and Worthing at 660VDC, third rail. Speeds of electric trains using third rail pickups were not recommended to travel above 50mph as the unevenness of the tracks caused loss of contact. Undeterred, on 1 January 1933, the Brighton line became the first electrified main line in the country.

ELECTRIFICATION SCHEMES • 59

Power unit. The LB&SCR also operated some services at 6.7kVDC. To haul the trains, they built some motor coaches. Here is No. 10112 Normally there were four coaches, with the power unit in the middle. (BPC)

London Bridge. A discerning reader will have a question – were both systems in operation at the same station at any time? The answer is 'yes' – here is London Bridge station with both direct current and alternating current systems. The lines immediately in front of our position have third rail whilst those beyond the huge signal box are for overhead wires. During that time, the SR extolled the virtues of this system as helping in the government's scheme for the relief of unemployment. The decision to abandon alternating current electrification was a curious one as it was this system that mainland Europe was investing in, as ultimately did the UK. The decision to go with 'live rail' was made in 1926, with the last alternating current trains running three years later. (BPC)

Portsmouth electrification scheme

The SR also used finances available in its new works project to continue its three-rail electrification programme along the South Coast from Brighton to Portsmouth. It was decided to electrify through to Portsmouth from London, by far the longest route attempted by the company. The scheme was announced in 1935; at this time the main line from Waterloo was electrified as far as Hampton Court Junction, so the scheme was to be from there via Woking and Guildford to Portsmouth Harbour. The lines to Portsmouth benefited greatly from electrification; traffic over the direct line, via Guildford, was particularly heavy, and the line sinuous and steeply graded. It had been difficult to work with steam power, but the gradients presented few problems for the electric trains. The new Portsmouth express multiple-units were made up of four coaches, so that three units were required to

Petersfield station. This view was taken from the footbridge, looking north. The platforms for Petersfield station are behind us with the Midhurst branch platform the other side of the road. Arriving is a steam hauled push-pull train. It has a coach at this end that has a special compartment at the front so that the engine driver can control the train. Later, when it had picked up the passengers waiting, the driver would walk to the ex-rear of the train, aboard the engine and set off for Midhurst. There was the end of three branch lines from stations that had electric services, Chichester (Portsmouth to Brighton), Petersfield (Portsmouth to Victoria) and Pulborough (Littlehampton to Christ's Hospital). (BPC)

Surbiton station. This was completely rebuilt in 1937 with two island platforms with SR designed canopies on the platforms. The buildings were designed by James Robb Scott in Art Deco style. (BPC)

form a twelve-coach train. On the Brighton line, twelve-coach trains consisted of two six-coach units. On the Portsmouth line it would have been wasteful to have provided three buffet cars so, for the first time in Britain, gangways were provided between units so that passengers could reach the restaurant car from any part of the train. This feature of the trains led to the units' official classification, 4-COR, meaning four-coach corridored (COR being the abbreviation) unit. The end gangways also led, indirectly, to another name. SR electric trains were fitted with a panel – until then located on unit ends between the two forward windows – on which a letter or number could be displayed to indicate the train's route. On these new units, the headcode indicator was placed where the offside front window would otherwise have been, as it was inconvenient to position it on the gangway door. This left only one forward window, that for the motorman, on the nearside. The resulting 'one-eyed' appearance and association with Portsmouth and the Royal Navy, inspired the unofficial epithet 'Nelsons', though the units were also known as 'Pompeys'.

Electric trains started running to steam train timings to Guildford from 3 January 1937, and Portsmouth and Southsea station was first reached by an electric service on 8 March 1937. There was a Royal Navy Fleet Review at Portsmouth on 20 May 1937, to commemorate the Coronation of King George VI and twenty twelve-car special electric trains ran between London and Portsmouth in addition to the ordinary steam service. However, end-to-end journey times, at 93–97 minutes, are not significantly different from 1937.

London, Midland and Scottish Railway (LMSR)

Many lines that fell into the LMSR orbit from 1923 especially those around Manchester, to Bury and Liverpool, and to Southport and Birkenhead, had long been electrified. Consequently there were only minor schemes during this time, mostly station improvements such as opening of Hillside station on the Liverpool to Southport line in 1926.

The Mersey railway was electrified in 1903. The 1936 works consisted of the introduction of six-car sets. However, the tunnel beyond Liverpool Central could not accommodate them and so the line in the tunnel was extended. This enabled trains to discharge passengers and then to shunt round to the opposite platform face at Liverpool Central, ready for the return on the other line. At that time, the small line was carrying 20 million passengers a year.

The LMSR worked on converting/connecting the Mersey line with the Wirral line so that the Wirral peninsula could connect with the city of Liverpool, in 1938.

New Brighton. A driver is passing the time of day with a passenger before returning to his driving compartment and setting off for Liverpool. Back from the sea was an extensive promenade. (BPC)

London and North Eastern Railway (LNER)

Tyneside

Manchester, Sheffield and Wath

When the government announced their scheme for the relief of unemployment, it certainly caught the LNER, on the hop. Whilst they had aspirations, they did not have any detailed plans for service improvements. Hastily, they drew up details for the electrification between Manchester, and Sheffield and Wath. The saga of electrification of this route is over twenty-five years in the telling until electric trains plied the line. In their wisdom, the pre-Grouping MS&LR, built a short section of line to connect two others in 1879. This through route enabled coal from Yorkshire to access the Woodhead tunnels and so into Lancashire with its factories and docks. There was only one problem with this connection; it was steeply graded, not to mention twisty, incorporated two tunnels and a viaduct – normal Yorkshire Dales terrain. To overcome the problems as time went on, the company, firstly the GCR then the LNER, simply put bankers onto the ends of the trains. This not only gave the train a shove up the bank but also protected against trains separating and running backwards down the slope.

Tyneside. In 1938, the LNER took advantage of the new finances to electrify the line south of the Tyne. As extra stock would be needed, the company decided to replace the aging units and to build two new parcels vans, in 1938. The new service needed eighteen two-car sets. Brand new Nos. 24235 and 24236 are seen here. (BPC)

64 • THE RAILWAY GROUPING 1923 TO THE BEECHING ERA

Above: **Worsbrough Bank, 1947.** The congestion on the line simply grew and grew. Whilst there was nothing new about this solution, what made the issue untenable in the long run is illustrated here. There are two engines banking the rear, often there were two at the front. Three engines at the rear was not uncommon. The line absorbed a vast number of train crews. Prior to the First World War, the GCR investigated ways of reducing costs by electrifying the line. They had some experience of this idea on their line at Shildon, near Newcastle. This led the company, now the LNER, to build the ultimate banker, seen earlier at the S&DR centenary celebrations. This monster had its own issues and ultimately it was not a permanent solution to the issue. The company reasoned that the problem was with a small section of freight only line from Wath marshalling yard to the eastern mouth of the Woodhead tunnel, which was causing problems. The company argued that this necessitated a different approach from the rest of the line from Manchester to Sheffield. As most railways did, a system of bankers was discussed to push the laden wagons up the Worsbrough incline. On reflection, had they executed this idea they could have done it sooner and would have saved the vast delay and expense involving the Woodhead tunnel. As it happens, there was a line with a similar problem in the North East of the country. Laden trains had to be taken to the docks, blast furnaces and iron works around Middlesbrough from the mines around Bishop Auckland. This started in 1915 and by the early 1930s the equipment needed extensive repair. Consequently, the whole class of ten engines were put into storage at Darlington. Their potential was never realised and apart from one being sent to Ilford, all were scrapped. The government's New Works Programme, to mop up unemployed men rather than the needs of this section of the railway system, probably won the argument. (H.C. Casserley)

Opposite above: **Banking locomotive.** As a part of the Manchester-Sheffield-Wath electrification it was proposed to convert the Shildon locomotives into banking engines. The English Electric Company Limited visited Darlington in September 1936 in order to assess their suitability. In 1941, No. 11 was moved to Doncaster Works for modification as a banking locomotive. Alterations included a more powerful set of motors giving a one-hour rating of 1,256hp and a total tractive effort of 37,600lb. Additional sandboxes and electric lights were fitted, and one central pantograph replaced the previous two. (BPC)

Opposite below: **New locomotive.** This was the first unit for the line. Its frames were laid at Doncaster in 1939 and after completion it underwent trials on the Manchester South Junction and Altrincham Railway (MSJ&AR), had a number change, and was put into storage at Doncaster. After a spell in Holland (1947–52) it received a number change and a nameplate from the Dutch, with affection. It would take until 1954 for the system to be operational from end to end. Originally, the Manchester, Sheffield and Wath system was to be made up of nine locomotives for express passenger trains, sixty-nine mixed traffic engines and ten banking engines. The outbreak of the Second World War forced a halt to electrification work and the order was reduced in November to just one locomotive. Having two bogies proved to be a big mistake. On starting there was a loss of pulling power on the leading axles resulting in wheel spin. If three axles had been adopted, then as they were destined to spend most of their time on heavy freight work, the wheel spin would have been much reduced and the resulting heavier locomotive would have helped in the braking sections on the descents on the Woodhead route. (RAS)

London, Midland and Scottish Railway (LMSR), and London and North Eastern Railway (LNER)

Old Trafford station. One of the anomalies of the Grouping was what to do with certain joint lines. Some were managed by joint committees. The (MSJ&AR) line, managed jointly by the LMSR and the LNER, ran the 8.5 miles from London Road, Manchester to Altrincham and carried large commuter traffic. This short, but intensively operated line was energised at 1,500VDC, following the recommendations of the Weir Committee on railway electrification and collection was from overhead wires using a pantograph. The Altrincham electrics provided a faster, more frequent service than the steam trains they had replaced and resulted in an 89 per cent increase in patronage on the line within the first five years. The new electric service also stimulated further suburban housing development close to the line and provided an early example of today's marketing slogans when the railway's publicists dubbed the initials MSJ&AR as 'Many Short Journeys and Absolute Reliability'. As a youngster I would often pass Warwick Road on the way to Trafford Park shed and have difficulty peering over the bridge as the road passes over the railway line, being too short. The station, taking the name of the road, opened on 11 May 1931. An Altrincham-bound three-car unit pauses at one of the four platforms, most essential on test match days at the adjacent Old Trafford ground. A section of the line, between Old Trafford and Sale, enabled all stations' electric trains to be overtaken by limited stations' stop trains. Also along the line were steam hauled trains between Manchester Central and Chester as well as steam hauled trains between London Road and Warrington Bank Quay. (BPC)

CHAPTER 10
THE RISE OF CARS AND LORRIES

Road transport grew rapidly during the 1920s, stimulated by the cheap sale of thousands of war-surplus vans and lorries. Also, the subsidised construction of new roads, which was mainly funded by local authorities, through rates and taxation, absorbed unemployed men. Meanwhile, new building and repairs to the railways, had to be paid for by the railways themselves. What was most worrying to the railway companies was the loss of freight to road haulage. This was largely because the government would not release the railways from their obligations as 'common carriers', which had been brought in the nineteenth century. It obliged railway companies to carry any cargo offered to it at a nationally agreed charge, which was usually well below a rate necessary to make the operation profitable for the railways. The intention had been to stop railway companies cherry picking the most profitable freight whilst refusing to carry less profitable items. This had been a necessary measure when railways had had an effective monopoly over land transport, but with road competition encroaching, it put the railways at a disadvantage, because they had to subsidise unprofitable freight operations with profitable ones, which drove up charges. Motor transport had become a fact of life following its usage in the First World War. Many men had been taught to drive during the war and when demobbed took advantage of cheaply disposed-of vehicles from the army to set themselves up as delivery firms. The road haulage operators, who

The rise of the motor vehicle. One-man-band delivery services using an ex-army lorry could undercut the rates charged by the railway companies and were much more flexible. Using their new skills and effectively a government subsidised vehicle, many men banded together to form firms that could challenge the railways companies' rates.

The railways fight back. Not to be outdone by these new motorised vehicles, the railways developed their own fleets of lightweight vehicles for deliveries. The railway companies had previously relied on horse-drawn trailers for local goods deliveries from the station; to compete they bought in motorised local delivery vehicles such as the Karrier 'Cob' and Scammell Mechanical Horse. These three-wheeler units were ideal for local collection and delivery services. With different types of trailers that could be detached, flexibility was the key word. Here small consignments could be delivered quicker than by horse and cart.

had no such restrictions, could privately negotiate any rate they wished to undercut the railways' published price lists, and take away their business while offering door-to-door delivery. It was then thought that no large railway could operate at a profit unless more than half of its traffic was freight, and thus any reduction in the freight business would also affect the viability of the passenger business.

The number of cars registered in 1930, was around 1 million and rising. During the 1940s the focus of production was centred on the war effort. While this may seem a large number it did not concern the railways too much as they were used for relatively short journeys. Without well maintained, direct trunk roads, the long distance motor coach only caused a ripple of unease. Registrations rose to 3 million in 1955.

The concept of the Scammell Mechanical Horse tractor unit with an easily detached articulated trailer was conceived in the early 1930s by D. Napier & Son. It had one front wheel in the midline. The LNER had approached D. Napier & Son for an answer to the problem of replacing horses for local haulage purposes, while retaining the flexibility of changing the wagons and the manoeuvrability of the horse and wagon. Production started in 1934 with a modified design which featured automatic trailer coupling and the single front wheel, which could be steered through 360°. There were two capable of pulling loads of 3 and 6 tons and each of the two sizes had a corresponding coupling size, which became known as the 3- and 6-ton coupling. The tractor units were powered by Scammell's own side valve petrol engine of 1,125cc in the 3-ton version and 2,043cc in the larger 6-tonner. The engine was offset to the left of the cab, which could cause stability problems in some circumstances, with units toppling over. The vehicles had manoeuvrability that was unmatched; it was possible to turn through 360° in under 20ft with a 16-ft trailer. The road speed of about 20mph suited the vehicle to local deliveries. The name arose because it was designed to get in and out of narrow twisty passages designed for a horse and cart and so they were a common and popular sight on the roads for the next twenty-five years.

The railway companies were not slow to augment their services or to replace horse-drawn vehicles with motorised ones to compete against carrier firms. A Royal Commission on Road and Rail Transport in 1931 was ineffectual at producing a solution. However, the subsequent Salter Report of 1933 was adopted as government policy; the Ministry of Transport lifted some of the restrictions on the railways while introducing licensing and safety regulations on hauliers. Against a storm of protest, the chancellor, Neville Chamberlain, significantly increased vehicle excise duty. However, just as the campaign looked like being successful, the Second World War started. The common carrier requirement was lifted by the Transport Act 1947.

Railway bus companies. Ironic as it may seem, bus companies sprang up to take people to railway stations; longer distance passenger travel was yet to come. Outside Southport station was a connecting bus service to nearby villages. Buses were useful to collect workers and ferry them to pitheads for the start of a shift, and to bring the finishing shift home.

DENNIS 26, 28 and 30 SEATER BUSES.
Write for Special Prices and Terms.

SPICERS MOTORS, LTD., SOUTHPORT.
Main Dennis Distributors and Coachbuilders. Telephone 2003.

CHAPTER 11
TRAINSPOTTING

Being 'directed' to work in the public relations department of the Southern Region seemed to be manna from heaven for the young Ian Allan. Quick, alert and knowledgeable about SR locomotives, he compiled a book about matters relating to the region's locomotives. Seeing that much of his task was supplying information about them for the public, he suggested that the company publish the information. When this was turned down, the 20-year-old eventually released his *ABC of Southern Locomotives* in 1942. Two hundred copies were printed, which could be bought from the compiler's home address for 1 shilling.

It nearly came to nought. When the CME of the company, Oliver V.S. Bulleid, received a complimentary copy, he demanded they be withdrawn or that Allan lose his job. Quite dramatic for a young man, he had the foresight to send a copy to the chairman of the company. This was enthusiastically received, and Allan was congratulated.

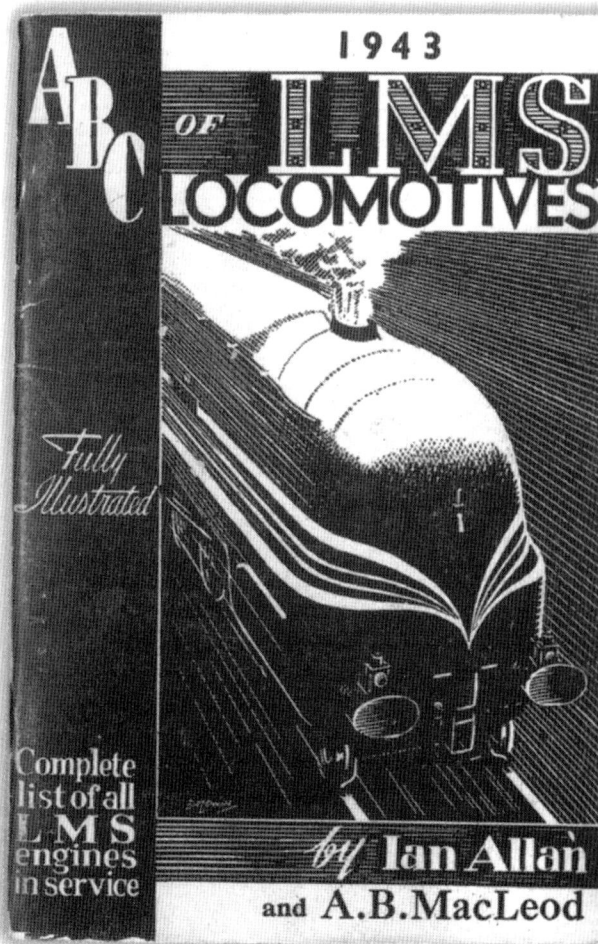

Right: **LMSR locomotives.** Despite war-time restrictions, on paper Allan's publications, including ones for the other members of the Big Four, followed and before the war ended he had left the SR to set up his own company, which later published magazines and books relating to all manner of railways, at home and abroad. Quite a brave move for a young man at those times. In fact, it is most likely that any reader of this book has at least one of Ian Allan's books on their shelves so widespread and popular have they become. At 'half a crown', books like these were quite expensive. However, so popular did trainspotting become that the success of the locomotive spotters' books was assured and a relatively cheap activity for the young (mostly lads) was born. In 1944, a group of schoolboy who were locomotive enthusiasts wandered on to the main line track, an incident which made headlines in the national newspapers. A code of conduct was required, and the ABC Ian Allan Locospotters' Club was formed, eventually attracting over 300,000 members the length and breadth of the country.

Opposite above: **Horseplay.** It is amazing what can be found in a car boot sales' 'odds' box. This is the end of Manchester Exchange station. Note the small group of youngsters at the ends of platforms. While sitting about on trolleys was a harmless activity and did not interfere with their business of the station, some lads messed about with the trolleys or their sheer numbers, which meant that at some stations they were banned from some platforms and elsewhere prohibited from going into the station. The tactic of buying a return ticket to the first station out overcame this. Many a ticket to Newton Heath I have bought and returned to Manchester Victoria taking in a round trip to the engine shed and returning via Dean Lane station. Happy days. The club became more popular when it organised special trains; parents were glad their children had found a safe activity to pursue. Crewe became a 'must go to' venue for trainspotters, yours truly included, due to the sheer number of services and different engines that used the station, let alone two very large engine sheds into which one tried to 'bunk'. Fortunately, a convenient footbridge not only served the fare-paying public but kept youngsters from the platforms.

Below: **Youthful pastime.** One over-riding concern of the railway companies was that the pastime could involve trespass, leading to injury or worse. There were calls to ban the activity and to burn the books. A small group of trainspotters watch as a V2 Class engine heads south on the GCR main line. This was an interesting place to observe trains as not only was there this line but to their left, at a lower level, is the ex-Midland line from Kirkby-in-Ashfield to Pye Bridge. I well remember observing trains in similar circumstances. My brother and I had made the short train ride to Newton-le-Willows from our Manchester home. A short distance east of the main Manchester to Liverpool main line was the Golborne to Winwick cut off of the West Coast Main Line. We had the best of both worlds, local trains on top and 'double-peg' expresses below. Fast forward to the more modern era and the activity has less allure for youngsters and more for older, often middle-aged men.

CHAPTER 12
POST-GROUPING INNOVATION

It is tempting to think of post First World War as a period of retrenchment on the railways. Nothing could be further from the truth. While the SR pressed ahead with electrification and dabbled with steam, and the other three companies explored new motive power, the prize was to run the fastest trains in the country.

Great Western Railway (GWR)

With its Castle and King engines dominating its express passenger trains as well as a range of engines for all other purposes, the GWR probably was keener on improving local services rather than new engines.

Diesel Railcars

The first generation units operated on the Banbury to Kingham line. Here is No. 10 at Sarsden Halt. The basic idea that the GWR had was for such railcars to supplement the existing steam traffic. However, so successful were they, with their limited seating, that they had to be replaced by steam-hauled trains! After the introduction of No. 18 with its trailing load it was shown that railcars could change a loss-making branch service into a profitable one. The railcars retained their ability to work stopping services on main line services when required. (Lens of Sutton)

In 1933, the GWR introduced the first of what was to become a very successful series of diesel railcars, which survived in regular use into the 1960s, when they were replaced with the new British first generation type diesel multiple unit (DMU). The designers realised that the successful 130bhp six-cylinder Associated Equipment Company (AEC) diesel engine, which was used in London buses, was capable, with some streamlined modifications, of operating a self-contained railcar. Experience from the popular 'Flying Hamburger' (Hamburg Flyer) diesel units operating in Germany led to the first prototype. After wind tunnel tests at the London Passenger Transport Board (LPTB) laboratory at Chiswick, the engine was transformed into a sleek streamlined body with alterations to the frontal area. Before completion, the railcar was bought by the GWR but before entering service, it was displayed at the International Commercial Motor Transport Exhibition at Olympia in November 1933. Such was the railcar's popularity at the exhibition it was estimated that over half of those who paid for admission to Olympia visited the railcar. Great publicity, something that the GWR thrived on, was also given to the railcar's movement from Olympia to the GWR sidings at Brentford when the exhibition closed.

Final design. The second batch had straight lines and flat panels against the previous curves and rounded surfaces. This was most noticeable on the lower part of the cab. This new design added 3ft to the overall length of the railcar, which had a seating capacity for forty-eight passengers. No. 17 was designed as an express parcels car; built in 1936 it had no seats and was capable of carrying 10 tons. The final railcars of the GWR series were operated as twin-coupled railcar units, the forerunner of today's DMUs. With the driving compartments situated at the outer ends of the set, buffet and toilet facilities could be provided for 104 seated passengers. However, if a standard corridor coach was installed between the 2 cars, seating numbers could be increased to 184. (BPC)

London, Midland and Scottish Railway (LMSR)

Articulated unit. In 1937 the LMSR built a modern diesel train. This was a three-car articulated railcar built to LMSR diagram No. D1996 and outshopped from Derby Carriage and Wagon Works in 1939. The cars were numbered 80000, 80001 and 80002. The streamlined three-car train was a single articulated unit; the two outer coaches were each 64ft long and rested on a centre coach that was 52ft long. A main line standard of performance was intended to have a maximum speed of 75mph. Accommodation in the end cars was split into two saloons with twenty-six seats in the outer saloon plus a lavatory, and twenty-eight seats in the inner saloon, all seats being reversible and third class. Between the outer saloon and the driving cab was a small luggage and brake compartment. The centre car was a composite with a thirty-seat third class saloon with a lavatory, and the other saloon having twenty-four first class seats. All of the seats were arranged as two plus two. The cab was generously proportioned with the driver in a central position. It entered revenue-earning service in 1939 based at Bedford and worked first on the line between Oxford (Rewley Road) and then on the St Pancras to Nottingham services. It was withdrawn on the outbreak of the Second World War in 1939, stored, and never re-entered passenger service. (Lens of Sutton)

London and North Eastern Railway (LNER)

Diesel shunters. Although humble, arguably one of the most important locomotives produced. Until the shunting of wagons ceased to be how the railways operated, small, short wheel based engines were the life blood of the marshalling yard and groups of sidings. All railway companies had them, often in large quantities – after nationalisation and standard engines emerged, this was the only type of engine not built, so successful were they. These were ordered at the LNER board meeting on 19 February 1941. They were built at the LNER's Doncaster Works, with the diesel-electric system supplied by The English Electric Company Limited. The resulting engines were virtually identical to similar LMSR engines. Four locomotives (Nos. 8000–8003) were built in 1944 and were originally classified as J45. They were then reclassified as DES1 (Diesel Electric Shunting 1) in September 1945. The four DES1s were renumbered as Nos. 15000–15003 between 1950 and 1952, spending most of their lives in Whitemoor Yard near March, Cambridgeshire. (R.K. Blencowe Negative Archive)

CHAPTER 13
COPING WITH HEAVIER TRAINS

Goods Engines

In the period of time that this book covers, practically all the country's energy needs were met by coal. It was either burnt for warmth or distilled into coal gas for warmth and lighting. All the companies that moved significant volumes of freight sought to maximise the length of their trains; much of this would be performed out of sight of the public and so most were unaware of the activity. Only the SR did not produce an engine beyond a 'mixed traffic' type.

Coal wagons. Vast quantities of the stuff were transported all over the country. This line of well-stocked wagons seems to stretch into the distance awaiting their disposal. The biggest flow of coal was to London and all four companies took part; the SR contribution was the smallest, mostly from the Kent coalfield. It is interesting to note that the three remaining railway companies evolved a convergence of design for their coal shifting engines. All of them adopted a chassis that consisted of eight driving wheels, with some also having a pony truck at the front to spread the weight of the engine. (BPC)

Great Western Railway (GWR)

Some of their biggest flows were to the docks in South Wales at Cardiff and Newport while another was to London. The construction of the Severn Tunnel shortened the latter journey, previously via Gloucester and Swindon, while with the Badminton line provided a direct line from the coalfield to London.

Welsh coal to London. At Severn Tunnel Junction there was a set of sidings where South Wales and Forest of Dean collieries sent their loaded coal wagons. Upon arrival, they were organised into lengths that could be sent down the 'hole'. To climb up the gradient on the English side, often needing bankers. The GWR practice was to have the two engines at the front of the train. A GWR 5101 Class engine pilots an unknown 4-6-0 engine as they set off for England. With the Severn Tunnel ahead, and a gradient against them, it would have taken all of the two footplate crew's skill to travel at a pace until they reach respite.

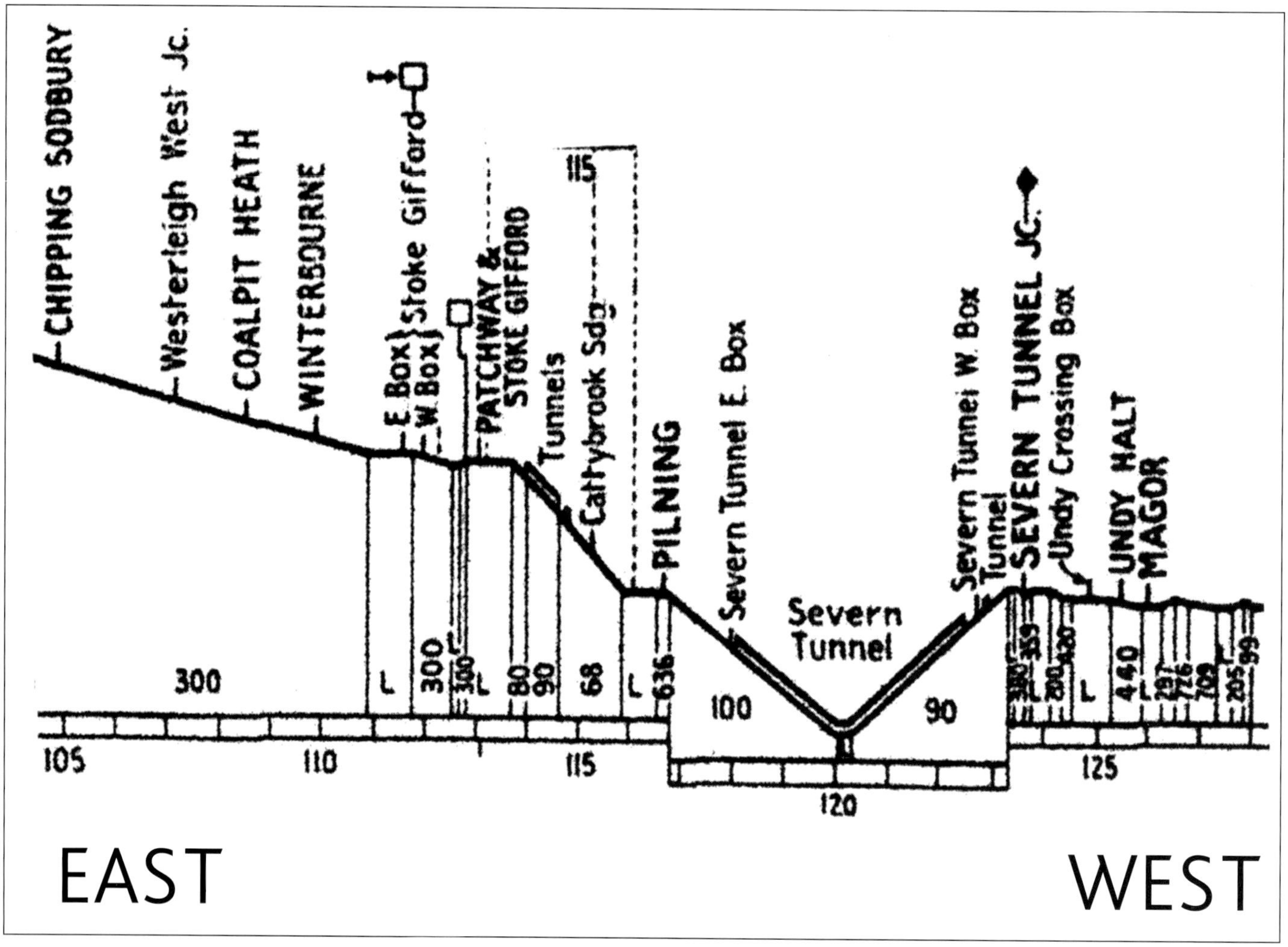

78 • THE RAILWAY GROUPING 1923 TO THE BEECHING ERA

Gradients. This diagram depicts the gradients faced by loaded trains, heading east, and empty trains heading west. It gives some idea of the struggle the footplate crews suffered on the up, to London, route. Only at Stoke Gifford (the site of Bristol Parkway now) was the incline manageable for one engine.

Two tunnel portals

Eastern end. This is the eastern end of the tunnel, near Pilning, on English soil. (BPC)

COPING WITH HEAVIER TRAINS • 79

Western end. This is the western end, near the Seven Tunnel. (BPC)

Below: **Hauling engine.** The company's most used engines for this traffic were their 28xx Class totalling thirty-five engines. The company built upon their success by assembling sixty-seven more starting in 1938. Here, in the last years of its existence, is No. 3812 coaled and standing in line at Reading shed, code 81D in its later years. (BPC)

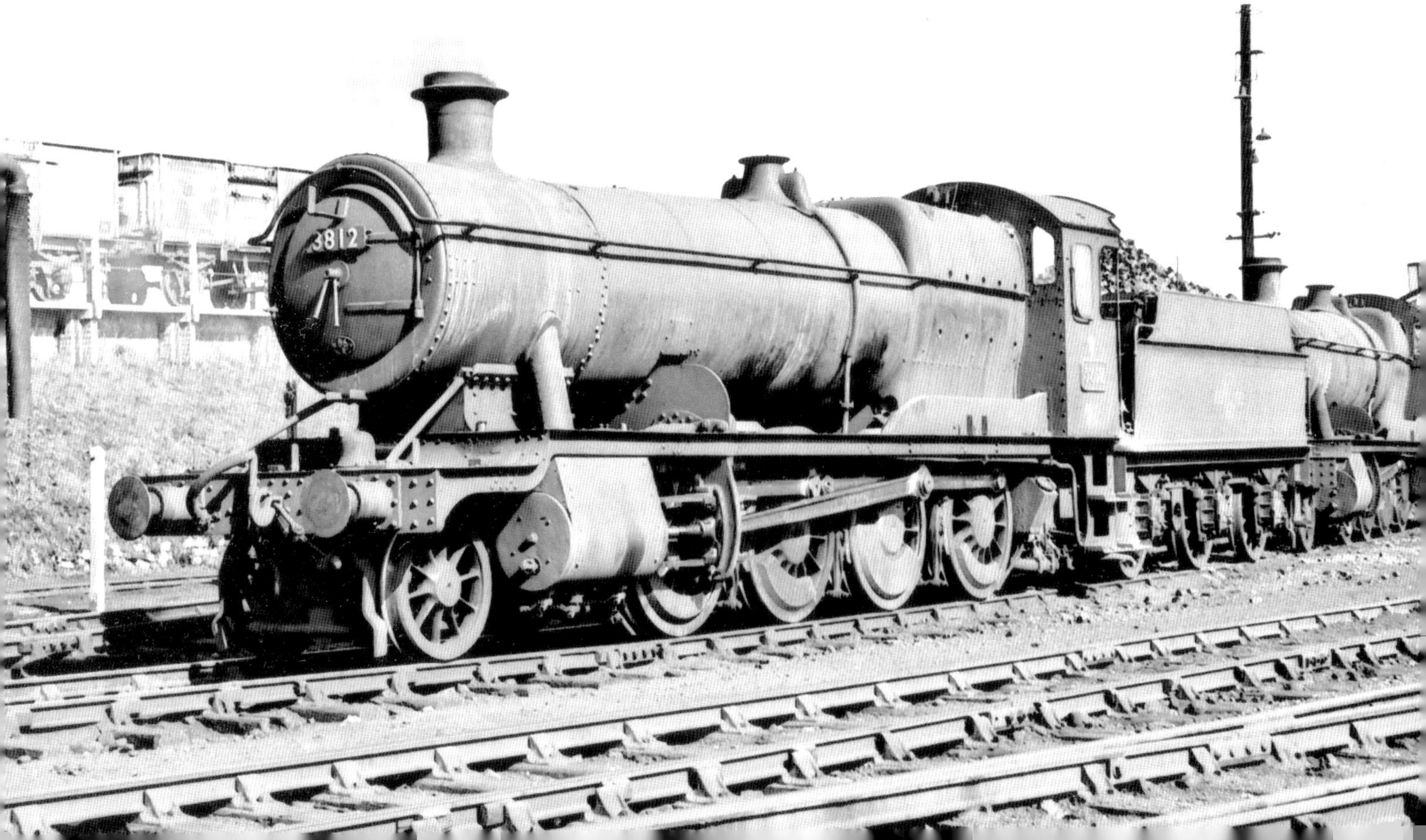

London, Midland and Scottish Railway (LMSR)

When the company was formed by the Grouping, it inherited many designs for moving freight trains. Those from the former MR tended to be six-coupled engines, whereas those from the former LNWR tended to be eight coupled. The smaller engines often needed to be double headed and so the new company, the LMSR, opted to replace worn out engines with the larger, eight coupled variety. The company introduced two variations of its successful G2 Class, one more successful than the other.

Beyer, Peacock and Company's Garrett engines. It is perhaps hard for us today with heat and power at the flick of a switch, to appreciate how dependent the country, commercially and domestically, was on coal. Taking one year, 1937, over 170 million tons of coal was moved around the country, much of it by rail. London was the greatest magnet, drawing in 2.5 million tons a year purely for household use. This company had two routes to London along two of its constituent companies, ex-MR from Toton to Cricklewood and ex-LNWR from Crewe to Willesden. The ex-MR route for coal to London was from its massive yard at Toton in Nottinghamshire. There, long coal trains, often double headed (although triple headed was not unknown) trains would set off for Cricklewood and Brent yard in North London. To reduce costs associated with the use of two train crews, the LMSR bought some of the articulated Garrett style locomotives from Beyer, Peacock and Company, and built at their works on the opposite side of the LNER main line through Gorton, Manchester. After 1928, the company began to use the name Beyer-Garratt to distinguish their locomotives. As engine No. 4970 shows, the Garratt design was basically two girders holding a boiler and a cab that were slung between two engine units, each with cylinders, wheels and motion. The weight of the locomotive was therefore spread over a considerable distance. Both engine units were topped by water tanks. The unit adjoining the cab end also held a fuel bunker. Three engines of this class were introduced experimentally in 1927 and were so successful that a further thirty were added three years later.

These engines would haul seemingly never-ending trains (90 loaded – 1,400 tons – at 20mph or 100 empty at 25mph), the lines being quadruple all the way. After their arrival, the trains would be divided and sent to local depots for use or distribution. Another major route was from the Hasland sidings in the Derbyshire coalfields, through the Peak District to Gowhole sidings prior to onward distribution to Manchester or Liverpool. The class then lasted twenty-five years, averaging 25,000 miles per year. However, the design did not age well, especially under wartime lack of maintenance, causing generally poor later opinions. (R.K. Blencowe Negative Archive)

Stanier freight locomotives. For almost forty years, William Stanier had been firmly ensconced in the ways of the GWR; after all, he did escort the engine to the USA in 1927. After set-up lunches with the top brass of the LMSR he was offered their top post from 1 January 1932. In almost a foretaste of the development of locomotives after the Second World War, Stanier was to provide a range of locomotives having the least possible number of classes that could operate all over the company's lines. The first examples were built in 1935 in a variety of works including The Vulcan Foundry Limited, North British Locomotive Company, Horwich, Beyer, Peacock and Company and this example, No. 8080, at Crewe. 126 built by 1939. After that time, the REC took over procurement for engines built in the Second World War. (BPC)

Coal for export, east and west

One of the lines that merged with others just before the Grouping was the Lancashire and Yorkshire. Apart from the cities it served, it connected the northern coalfields to the docks in Liverpool in the west, and at Goole in the east. Large engines were needed to haul the often 1,000-ton trains.

From colliery to sorting sidings. To haul these massive trains, large boilered engines such as No. 52916 were necessary. It is seen here at Aintree's sorting sidings. As there was very little storage space at Liverpool's docks, trains were stored at Aintree and their wagons tripped to their destination. This was often performed on the High Level Coal Railway in Liverpool's docks by one of the pre-Grouping L&RY 'Pugs'. They ferried loaded coal wagons between the sidings and the docks with empty wagons performing the reverse. The cramped nature of the lines here meant these engines were always scurrying about pushing and pulling wagons. (H.C. Casserley)

London and North Eastern Railway (LNER)

The company had two routes for hauling coal to London, the GNR line from Doncaster and the GER line from Whitemoor. In an attempt to reduce the number of loaded coal trains, the LNER decided to increase the length of its trains up to eighty wagons, around 1,300 tons. However, in 1932 congestion on the GNR main line was becoming a serious problem, and a move towards reducing the number of slow moving coal trains was made. One solution was to haul smaller, sixty wagon, trains with faster, K3 Class engines.

Journey's end. Many of the coal trains ended up here at Ferme Park, near Harringay. What a vast undertaking. In the distance is the GNR station with its characteristic long footbridge. On the right is the coaling tower of Hornsey engine shed. The main lines run through the middle of the station with extensive goods sidings in front of our position and over to the right. In the middle is a flyover and in the background is the mechanism for coaling engines, nicknamed cenotaphs, at Hornsey engine shed. This was an 1928/29 improvement and had two bunkers which could hold 200 tons. While witnessing the hoisting up of loaded coal wagons and their emptying into the bunkers in an almighty crash, it must have caused a Hornsey dust to cover the nearby houses. However, it did enable engines to be coaled much more quickly than by hand. Of the seventy engines allocated there on the last day of the LNER in 1947, tank engines were predominant for shunting the sidings. (BPC)

Passenger engines

It was the engines that hauled the express trains that gleamed at the platform ends which gave the company publicity. All the Big Four developed larger engines in response to the heavier, more numerous vehicles that made up trains. The boardroom agenda was to capture the accolade, 'world's fastest train'. To haul the longer and heavier trains needed more powerful locomotives.

Some members of the Big Four, namely the GWR (Castle Class from 1923 and King Class engines since 1927), the SR (Lord Nelson Class since 1926), the LNER 4-6-2 (A3 Class since 1927) had been steadily introducing their own large engines for express haulage, leaving the LMSR rather out on a limb in the competitive sphere.

One of the reasons for this is that of all the new companies, the LMSR stood, not entirely alone, in having internal battles to solve before it could move on. This in turn was a consequence of all having large powerful companies and their management teams having to all sit round the same table and sing from the same hymn sheet; needless to say, this took time to be resolved before a coherent body could examine how it could move forward outside the boardroom now that its internal issues had been resolved. It was not until the LMSR persuaded Stanier to leave the GWR and move to become the CME of the LMSR in 1932 that the products of Crewe bore fruit.

Great Western Railway (GWR)

Of the four 'big' railway companies after the Grouping, the GWR was the first, by some margin, to produce an engine capable of hauling its heaviest express trains.

Castle Class. When Charles Benjamin Collett took over as CME at the GWR in 1922, he looked at the issue of more powerful engines than a Star Class engine (which would have pushed them over the 20-ton axle weight limit) not by having a bigger boiler but having a different steam generating apparatus – a newly designed No. 8 boiler which was both larger and lighter while remaining within the axle limit. The company used the first engine of its new Castle Class 4-6-0 locomotive, No. 4073 *Caerphilly Castle* in August 1923. The elegantly curved and distinctive external steam pipes made them easily identifiable, and the introduction of a side cab window was a great aid for the footplate crew. This class of engine was not the first 4-6-0 style engine that company owned (they already had the Star Class) but somehow for only a small percentage increase in weight (6 per cent) the designers had been able to increase its power output by 14 per cent, a distinct advantage in a competitive era. Part of this is due to larger grate area (8 per cent) and greater heating surfaces (12 per cent). Built at Swindon, the initial batch of ten continued a number series unbroken from the Star Class. Fifty such engines were built in the same decade, almost before the other three (of the Big Four) were out of the starting gates. (BPC)

King Class. The GWR's general manager, Sir Felix Pole, recognised that if the company wanted its heaviest trains to be fast then the weight limits imposed upon designers would have to be investigated. It would have been easier to have a larger boiler engine, but the extra weight would have restricted its use to only certain routes. The designer, Charles Benjamin Collett, explored the idea of a 'super' Castle Class, which would have the desired power and following a series of bridge renewals on main lines, allowed the weight limit to be raised to 22.5 tons. Frederick W. Hawksworth, the chief draughtsman of the GWR in Swindon, raised the boiler pressure to 250lb/sq.in, increased the cylinder stroke from 26 to 28in with slightly smaller driving wheels (78in) than the 'Castle' (80.5in). These factors together had the effect of increasing the tractive effort.

Twenty locomotives were ordered from the GWR's Swindon Works in 1927 (lot 243). The first locomotive, No. 6000 *King George V*, appeared in June 1927. It was followed by five others, Nos. 6001–6005, a month later. The remaining fourteen (6006–6019) appeared at regular intervals between February and July 1928. A second batch of ten locomotives, Nos. 6020–6029 (lot 267), appeared between May and August 1930. No. 6007 *King William III* was written off after an accident near Shrivenham on 15 January 1936 and was condemned on 5 March. A replacement was built (lot 309), which may have incorporated some parts from the damaged locomotive; it took the same number and name and was added to stock on 24 March 1936. It was originally intended that the class be named after notable cathedrals but following an invitation to feature a GWR locomotive in the Baltimore and Ohio Railroads' centenary celebrations, the GWR decided to make them more notable by naming the class after British kings. The class proved to be successful and able to cope with the heaviest express trains at a higher-speed timetable average than the Castle Class.
(R.K. Blencowe Negative Archive)

Southern Railway (SR)

Lord Nelson Class. Strictly speaking, the King Arthur Class has its origins in pre-Grouping times. The LSWR built their N15 Class from 1918 to haul their heaviest express trains to the South Coast ports and to Exeter. Following the Grouping of companies in 1923, the LSWR became part of the SR and its publicity department gave the N15 locomotives names associated with Arthurian legend; the class hence becoming known as King Arthur. Although the later King Arthur Class engines could haul the company's express trains on the main line towards Exeter, there were other demands on the locomotive stock. By the mid-1920s, the SR's traffic department wanted to start operating heavier loads at sustained speeds of 55mph so as not to impede the congested electrified lines around London. However, any enlargement of the existing two-cylinder design was not possible due to weight restrictions imposed by the railway's civil engineers' department. Although principally designed by their CME in 1926 for Continental boat trains from London Victoria, they were also later used for express passenger work to the south-west of England. Sixteen of them were constructed, representing the most powerful (although not the most successful) SR design. They were all named after famous admirals. Built at Eastleigh in 1929 No. 864 *Sir Martin Frobisher* was built at Eastleigh in 1929. The chimney would eventually be replaced by a squat Lemaître variety. The prototype named *Lord Nelson* appeared in August 1926. It was tested on a variety of duties over the next year, with sufficiently encouraging results for an initial order for ten more locomotives for delivery between May 1928 and April 1929 to be placed. These were originally scheduled to be allocated to the company's chief depot to serve Victoria station, Battersea depot (Stewarts Lane) and fitted with 4,000 gallon six-wheeled tenders suitable for the Continental ports. However, during construction, it was decided to equip half of the class with 5,000 gallon eight-wheeled tenders necessary for the longer west of England routes and to allocate them to Nine Elms depot. Eventually all were so equipped. A further batch of ten locomotives was ordered in 1928, before the previous batch had been delivered, but when it became apparent that trading conditions after the financial crash of 1929 would be likely to reduce the demand for Continental travel, this second order was reduced to five. (Lens of Sutton)

London, Midland and Scottish Railway (LMSR)

Royal Scot Class. Rumour – and railway circles are no less prone to such matters than others – has a back story to this issue. Speculation has it that having their eyes opened to what was happening in the world outside theirs, in early 1927, the LMSR asked to borrow a set of drawings for a Castle Class engine from the GWR. Getting short shrift to such an audacious proposal, they then approached another of the Big Four. Now the LNER, with its Pacific A3 Class engine making leaps along the East Coast was hardly likely to gift an own goal to its competitor, albeit on the West Coast. That only left the SR. With everything to gain they loaned a set of plans for their Lord Nelson 4-6-0 engine. If only the LNWR had the capacity, waiting, to build such engines, the saga would have ended here. They did not, and so sub-contracted it out to the North British Locomotive Company in Glasgow. The order was for fifty engines and the time frame was as soon as possible. As the original engines only had little chance to show their worth, this was something of a gamble by the LMSR board. As it happens, all were delivered before the end of the year – quite an impressive showcase for the North British Locomotive Company. The design's large, parallel boiler and squat chimney broke with the tradition in the company of having a strong Midland influence. However, the livery was crimson lake (or Midland red as some would have it) with large (18in) running numbers on the sides of the tender. The old Midland influence would not go away as it asserted itself in the small size tender to Henry Fowler (CME of the MR in the years leading to the Grouping) pattern. This was rectified, in 1936 by being paired with tenders originally intended for Jubilee Class engines, capable of holding 4,000 gallons of water.

Some of the engines had hardly drawn carriages when at the end of 1927 the decision was made to remove the running numbers to the cab side and have LMS on the side of the tender. However, to have the numbers and letters all at the same height and size, they were reduced to 14in.

Six people, including the driver and fireman, died at an accident at Leighton Buzzard in 1931. Their train, the down Royal Scot was transferring from the fast line to the slow line. Due to the derailment and loss of life, it was impossible to reach a conclusion as to its cause. The train was not excessively speeding but the distant and home signals may have been ignored due to smoke and steam on the cab window. As a result side deflector plates were fitted to all members of the class. Later variations having the upper part being angled inwards. Experiments were tried with other smaller smoke deflectors, and in fact, the SR were also trying out similar trials. Chimneys were altered in the early 1940s. So successful were these engines that another twenty were built at the Derby workshops in 1930. (Gordon Coltas Collection)

Princess Royal Class. Upon arrival at the LMSR in 1932, William Stanier brought with him some Swindon practices. This resulted in a small class of twelve engines (the Princess Royal Class) to augment the Royal Scot Class of engine in their delivery of the famous Royal Scot train between London and Glasgow. Stanier argued that as good as the GWR's King Class of engine was, for the longer journeys on the LMSR, a larger firebox was needed necessitating a pair of trailing wheels to support it. This broadside view amply illustrates this idea and leads the reader to support the idea of the time, probably put about by the LMSR publicity department, that these engines were, 'the largest and most powerful locomotives in Great Britain'. Several more of this class were pencilled in (Nos. 6213–6219) but they were eclipsed by the need for competing LNER engines as streamlined Coronation Class engines. No. 6201. (BPC)

London and North Eastern Railway (LNER) Pacific

More than ten years before the Grouping the railway company, the GNR was responsible for running express trains up the East Coast Main Line. They were chiefly hauled by Atlantic style engines with large boilers, developed by their engineer, Henry Alfred Ivatt. When Nigel Gresley succeeded to that post in 1911, he was aware that the policy was reaching its limits and more powerful engines were needed. The intention was to produce an engine able to handle, without assistance, main line express services. However, his initial design of 1915 of an elongated version of the existing Atlantic design, had four cylinders. After studying American (Pacific wheel arrangement) designs gave Gresley the impetus to produce his own design, dating from 1922, just on the cusp of formation of the Big Four. This design replaced the trailing truck of the Atlantic arrangement with a driving wheel so designating them Pacific wheel arrangement. Following the first two GNR Pacifics, introduced in 1922, the GNR board ordered a further ten 1470-Class locomotives (Class A1), which were under construction at Doncaster at the time of the formation of the LNER in 1923.

The route to fame. One of the group, No. 1472 *Flying Scotsman* was chosen to attend the 1925 Railway Centenary Exhibition where the company boasted it was, 'the largest and most powerful express passenger engine in Great Britain'; its number was altered to No. 4472. With modified valve gear, this locomotive was one of five Gresley Pacifics selected to haul the prestigious non-stop Flying Scotsman train service that went from London to Edinburgh, hauling the inaugural train on 1 May 1928. Pictured at King's Cross shed, getting ready, the locomotives ran with a new version of the large eight-wheel tender, which held 9 tons of coal. This and the usual facility for water replenishment from the water trough system between the railway tracks enabled them to travel the 392 miles (631km) from London to Edinburgh in eight hours, non-stop. The tender included a corridor connection and tunnel through the water tank giving access to the locomotive cab from the train to permit replacement of the driver and fireman without stopping the train. Engine No. 4472 became the first steam locomotive to be officially authenticated at 100mph on 30 November 1934, driven by Bill Sparshatt and running a light test train. It earned a place in the land speed record for railed vehicles; the publicity conscious LNER made much of the fact. The locomotive ran with its corridor tender between April 1928 and October 1936, after which it reverted to the original type; in July 1938 it was paired with a streamlined non-corridor tender. It has taken the role of the most famous steam locomotive, if not one of the most famous locomotives in the world. Awaiting its time is LNER No 4472 *Flying Scotsman* undergoing its final preparations at King's Cross shed. Its train will be the first 392 miles non-stop run between London and Edinburgh on 1 May 1928. (BPC)

CHAPTER 14
STREAMLINED ENGINES

There were many attempts at high speed running by the railway companies, noticeably in the early 1930s. The Bristolian and Cheltenham flyers spring easily to mind. While it would not be possible to list, in detail, all such titled trains, I have tried to illustrate the phenomena by selected examples. As in any pictorial account, the availability of illustrations limit the survey. Whilst some companies had large powerful engines for example, GWR's Castle and King classes, and the SR with its heavy boat trains hauled by Lord Nelson Class engines, there were two that acutely competed with each other for the title of 'fastest train in the world'. Generally speaking, most companies' named trains ran from London to the largest city in its area, there being over fifty such trains in the two decades, although not all ran at the same time, and some only lasted a short time.

Great Western Railway (GWR)

The streamlining of GWR locomotives was a less than enthusiastic attempt to get on the bandwagon that both the LNER and the LMSR adopted. Although not in a bad financial state, the company saw no reason to spend excessively on a fringe activity.

No. 6014 *King Henry VII*. This was a King Class 4-6-0 steam locomotive that was built at GWR's Swindon Works in May 1928. It was fitted with streamlining from March 1935, but all was removed by January 1943 except for the V-shaped cab. The engine was partially streamlined in March 1935 with a hemispherical smokebox door, continuous splashers, straight nameplate and a swept-back cab front. However, the appendages were soon removed, with the exception of the cab. No. 6014 was one of the locomotives that received for a brief period some bizarre streamlining with a bulbous smokebox and a tapered cowling behind the chimney. Whilst both the LNER and later the LMSR streamlined their main express locomotive class, Charles Benjamin Collett was obviously not enamoured by the publicity department's request for the GWR to adopt a similar practice. Although most of the 'streamlining' was removed, the V-shaped front to the cab was retained. Also, because of the engine's inability to carry reporting numbers (introduced from 1934 onwards) on the smokebox front in its streamlined condition, a special frame for these numbers had to be made to be carried above the buffer plank. (BPC)

To haul trains over long distances rapidly, powerful locomotives are needed. Both of the competing companies competing for Anglo-Scottish traffic produced new designs for their new trains streamlining basically existing engines.

London, Midland and Scottish Railway (LMSR)

With the mood changing in the LMSR camp there was a clamour, possibly hastened by events in Doncaster, that the way to claim top prize was to have non-stop travel between London and Glasgow. Consequently, the Coronation Class engines were designed and built at Crewe. They were an enlarged and improved version of Stanier's previous design, the Princess Royal Class, and on test were the most powerful steam locomotives ever used in Britain at just over 2,500 horsepower. The locomotives were specifically designed for power as it was intended to use them on express services between London Euston and Glasgow Central; their duties were to include the hauling of a proposed non-stop express, subsequently named the Coronation Scot. Five of these ten were specifically set aside to pull the Coronation Scot.

An unusual feature of all Coronation Class tenders was that they were fitted with a steam-operated coal pusher to bring the coal down to the firing plate. When this was in operation, a plume of steam could be seen rising from the rear face of the coal bunker backwall. This equipment greatly helped the locomotive's fireman to meet the high physical demands on long journeys.

When first painted, the LMSR topcoats for the Coronation Class came in two basic colours, Caledonian blue and crimson lake. Linings for streamliners involved the renowned 'speed whiskers' consisting of stripes emerging from the centre of the front of the locomotive to run in parallel along the sides. The first five locomotives, Nos. 6220–6224, were painted in Caledonian blue.

The second and fourth batches of streamlined locomotives, Nos. 6225–6229 and 6235–6244, were painted in crimson lake. The LMSR shop grey was carried briefly in service on No. 6229 *Duchess of Hamilton* from 7 September 1938 until its return to Crewe

No. 6222 *Queen Mary*. Appears here in blue livery, entering Crewe station. (BPC)

Works later that year. It was then painted crimson lake and disguised as No. 6220, in preparation for the 1939 visit to the New York World's Fair. Lettering and numerals for both Caledonian blue and crimson lake liveries were in a newly created style of unshaded sans-serif. The LMSR was as mindful as the LNER regarding publicity. Whilst the latter had attained the speed record, the LMSR reasoned that with some modifications other records may be withing their grasp. An earlier test indicated that the locomotive's power was compromised by its single blastpipe. Consequently, a double blastpipe and chimney were installed and on 26 February 1939, a retest was undertaken. The engine hauled a train of twenty coaches, including a dynamometer car, from Crewe to Glasgow and back. Even though the load was 620 tons, the train was hauled up the climbs to the summits at both Shap and Beattock at unprecedented speeds. Drawbar horsepower, representing the power conveyed directly to the twenty-coach train, was frequently over 2,000hp and a maximum of 2,511hp was recorded. This remains the official British record for a steam locomotive to this day. Experts estimated that the horsepower at the cylinders was between 3,209 and 3,333hp. Although this was on a test run with two fireman and so it is unlikely this level of performance could be repeated on a daily basis, the LMSR basked in attaining the British power record.

London and North Eastern Railway (LNER)

The Class A4 is a group of streamlined engines designed by Nigel Gresley for the LNER in 1935. He assessed the performance of the fast diesel trains in Germany and saw no reason why steam could not do equally well with a decent fare-paying load behind the locomotive.

Papyrus. Following trials in 1935, the A3 Pacific style No. 2750 *Papyrus*, pictured here at Grantham, recorded a new maximum of 108mph (173.8km/h) and completed the journey to Newcastle in under four hours. The LNER's chief general manager, Ralph Wedgwood, authorised Gresley to produce a streamlined development of the A3, designated it A4 Class. (R.K. Blencowe Negative Archive)

SILVER LINK LOCOMOTIVE.

***Above, below, opposite above and opposite below*: A4 Class.** Initially four locomotives were built in 1935, all with the word 'silver' in their names. The first was No. 2509 *Silver Link*, followed by No. 2510 *Quicksilver*, No. 2511 *Silver King* and No. 2512 *Silver Fox*. (BPC, R.K. Blencowe and J. Suter)

To improve the engine's performance, several alterations were made, including higher boiler pressure and an alteration to the firebox chamber, all of which contributed to a more efficient locomotive than the A3; consumption of coal and water were reduced. The class was noted for its design, which not only improved its aerodynamics, increasing its speed capabilities, but also created an updraught to lift smoke away from the driver's line of vision, a problem inherent in many steam locomotives. Fitting smoke deflectors was an alternative solution, but it would have destroyed the iconic shape.

CHAPTER 15
ENGLAND'S FIRST STREAMLINED TRAIN

To many readers, even the mildly curious, is the topic of 'What did the railways do between the wars?' and they don't usually mention streamlining and the rivalry between companies on the London to Scotland services.

The first streamlined service. The Silver Jubilee was run by the LNER to celebrate the twenty-fifth year of George V's reign, 1935. During a press run to publicise the service, the hauling engine, *Silver Link*, twice achieved a speed of 112.5mph, breaking the British speed record and sustained an average of 100mph over a distance of 43 miles. The Silver Jubilee train commenced service on 30 September 1935, the train travelling between London King's Cross and Newcastle. The train was painted silver throughout. It was composed of two twin-set articulated coaches, and one triplet-set, seven coaches in all. The Silver Jubilee flyer was a trail blazer. In the first place, it was booked to cover 536.6 miles every day – from Newcastle to London and back – at an inclusive average speed of 67.1mph in spite of severe slowings, through Peterborough, Selby and York, and minor slacks elsewhere. This entirely new train – locomotive and coaches – had been built with streamlining from tip to tail.

A young boy, and a couple of friends who are trainspotting at the trackside must have had a surprise. From their vantage point they would know of the impending arrival of the express when the signalman pulled the appropriate levers for a double-peg. Having probably experienced this situation on previous occasions, they took the warning of the express in their stride and probably chattered nonstop about which engine it would be. To their amazement, leading to jaw-dropping moments, it wasn't an A3 Pacific but a streamlined engine with coaches to match, glistening in the sun, flashing past their position. When the dust had settled one would say, 'Did you see that? A silver bullet streaking. What was it? Will we see it on the return? Will it pull the same train tomorrow? Wait till we tell them at school, they won't believe us.' It would take more than bread and jam at tea-time for the boys to calm down around the table at home, later. (BPC)

Following the commercial success of the Silver Jubilee train, other streamlined services were introduced.

The Coronation. This ran between London and Edinburgh from July 1937, stopping at Newcastle and here at York. The northbound train left London at 4.00 pm and arrived in Edinburgh six hours later. The southbound train ran half an hour later. Whereas the progenitor of the streamlined trains, Silver Jubilee, was painted silver, this was painted a two-tone blue livery (garter blue). The eight coaches were in four two-car articulated sections and the A4 Pacific locomotive, also in blue, had red wheels. (R. Joy)

The West Riding Limited. This linked Bradford and Leeds-London and return, September 1937 for which more A4s were built. Eventually, thirty-five of the class were built to haul express passenger trains on the East Coast Mail Line route from London via York to Newcastle and later via Newcastle to Edinburgh. The company built a new set of carriages, identical to the Coronation sets of 1935 which comprised four twin articulated coaches with two kitchen cars in each train set. There were seats for 48 first-class and 168 third-class passengers. (BPC)

Tenders. The A4 Class locomotives were known by trainspotters as 'streaks'. Although the engine *Mallard* is credited with a world speed record (126mph) on a run in July 1938, it was targeted to be surpassed in September the following year with a prospect of 130mph being achievable. However, the outbreak of the Second World War prevented this. The desire to have non-stop running from London to Edinburgh was deemed too much for one set of footplate crew and so a unique feature was devised to achieve a crew-changeover without stopping. The standard tender was modified by reducing the water capacity of the tender and building a narrow corridor (18in wide) connecting the footplate with the first coach. As there were several water troughs along the route the engine could easily replenish its supply so there was little chance of the water carrying capacity of the tender becoming a problem. (BPC)

The most striking feature of the design is the streamlining. From the buffer beam, a casing across the width of the engine rises in a curve to the top level of the boiler, and merges at the rear end into the wedge-fronted cab. The cab roof is prolonged over the front of the tender, with a flexible connexion between, so that the engine-crew is completely enclosed. The casing on either side of the engine covers the cylinders and sweeps back to the cab in a more gradual curve. The front end of the locomotive thus resembles a gigantic wedge cutting through the atmosphere.

It is in view of the exceptional speed and comfort provided by the Silver Jubilee, that a supplementary fare over and above the ordinary ticket was made for its use. The charge was 5 shillings to first-class and 3 shillings to third-class passengers. For many years past the only 'extra fare' trains in Great Britain have been those composed exclusively of Pullman cars; but the Silver Jubilee represented a definite inquiry by the LNER as to whether the British public really did desire facilities of this description.

Sections of automatic signalling were installed between Newcastle and York and the distances between signals are comparatively short, so that it was essential here to restrict the running speed to a little over 70mph. For this reason, it was necessary slightly to amend the original schedule and to allow 3½ minutes more between York and Darlington, with a corresponding acceleration between King's Cross and York.

CHAPTER 16
RIVALRY IN THE HIGH SPEED ERA OF THE 1930s

Streamlined coastal contest

1937 was very important to the two railway companies that ran services from London to Scotland. While the LMSR ran to Glasgow, the LNER went to Edinburgh. Just to make life confusing, one (to Glasgow) was titled, The Coronation Scot while to Edinburgh one called The Coronation; both were inaugurated in 1937, the year of King George VI's crowning. Just to confuse the reader even more, one of the LMSR engines, which hauled the Coronation Scot, carried the name Coronation. While most of trains ran in isolation, these two were in competition for the 'fastest train in the world' title, along the London to Scotland route.

I have tried to select a small handful to show these exciting engines at speed in an attempt to take the reader back to lineside days as the trains sped past.

The Coronation Class of express passenger engines were designed by William Stanier. They were an enlarged and improved version of his previous design, the Princess Royal Class, and on test, were the most powerful steam locomotives ever used in Britain at 2,511hp. The locomotives were specifically designed for power as it was intended to use them on express services between London and Glasgow. Their duties were to include the hauling of a proposed non-stop express, subsequently named the Coronation Scot. The first ten locomotives of the Coronation Class were built in a streamlined form in 1937 by the addition of a steel streamlined casing. Five of these ten were specifically set aside to pull the Coronation Scot.

Publicity poster for Scottish services. Notice how the two companies have tried to keep to their own timetables rather than to out-do each other. So the LMSR has a unified departure time of 1.30pm and arrival time of 8pm where as the LNER is content to bask in the shorter journey time. To be honest, with a shorter route and less steeply graded they were always going to win that race. (BPC)

***Above*: Lichfield Trent Valley station.** Tearing through the middle line at Lichfield Trent Valley station in 1939 is No. 6225 *Duchess of Gloucester* in crimson lake livery. (E.R. Morten)

***Below*: Whitmore troughs.** Collecting water, at speed, on Whitmore troughs is No. 6221 *Queen Elizabeth* in blue livery. (E.R. Morten)

Although a later batch of five unstreamlined locomotives was produced in 1938, most of the ensuing Coronation Class were outshopped as streamliners. As well as their streamlined shape, the painting of lines along the red or blue background from the front of the locomotive along the sides and tenders was a visual stroke of genius causing heads to turn when they streaked passed.

It was customary on all British main line journeys to change engines at convenient locations to avoid the lengthy process of re-coaling. The Coronation locomotives were therefore strategically stationed at key points between London and Glasgow, and they would be assigned to the shed at that location. The chosen locations were at London (Camden shed), Crewe (Crewe North), Carlisle (Upperby) and Glasgow (Polmadie).

London and North Eastern Railway (LNER)

No other British steam locomotives have a longer or more consistent record of high speed running than the A4s. Instances of 100mph running by them must exceed those of all other types combined, though 90mph was a relatively rare event with steam traction, much less 100mph. Their home territory – the East Coast Main Line – has more opportunities for high speed running (particularly Stoke Bank) than any other in the UK. In August 1936, the Silver Jubilee train on the descent of Stoke Bank headed by No. 2512 *Silver Fox* achieved a maximum of 113mph, then the highest speed attained in Britain with an ordinary passenger train. Although A4s were primarily designed

New Southgate. Racing past New Southgate is No. 4462 *Great Snipe*, a name it carried until 1937 when it was altered to *Golden Fleece*. (RAS)

Near Hatfield. No. 4489 *Woodcock* speeds through. It too underwent a name change in 1937 to *Dominion of Canada* when it acquired a bell on the front. (RAS)

for high speed express work, they were also capable of high power outputs. In 1940, No. 4901 *Capercaillie* exerted 2,200hp, admittedly on flat track, north of York, hauling twenty-one coaches at an average speed of 75.9mph for 25 miles. The highest recorded power output from an A4 was 2,450hp when *Mallard* was hauling eleven coaches (390 tons tare, 415 tons gross) up Stoke Bank at a sustained 80mph in 1963.

West country rivalry

Both the GR and the R ran express services from London to Exeter. Thence the GWR trains continued to Plymouth along the Channel coastal route and went on to Penzance. The SR also had a line to Plymouth as well as many towns on the 'Ocean Coast'.

Opposite above: **Atlantic Coast Express.** Using posters with concepts such as, 'Ocean Coast Express' the SR wanted to beat its rival, the GWR for the traffic by using restaurant cars and powerful locomotives. Here is the N15 Class *Sir Gawaine* when the service first started in 1926. As can be seen from the poster, it carried through coaches for a variety of West Country towns. Motive power for the 11.00 am from Waterloo altered when the Lord Nelson, a much more powerful class of engine, soon took over the running with ever more coaches to haul. The title of the train originated from a competition the company ran amongst its employees for the service; a guard from Woking won. With attempts to speed up the service one would have thought that a non-stop to Exeter from London would have been the order of the day. However, the track layout at Salisbury precluded this had, in fact, caused a derailment there some twenty years earlier. From then, also with no water troughs on its network, SR trains were forced to stop there to replenish their water tanks. (BPC)

Opposite below: **Union Castle, 1949.** Here is the Merchant Navy Class No. 21C2 at Exmouth Junction shed on 'ACE' duties with the fireman trimming the coal in the tender. When Oliver V.S. Bulleid took over as CME of the SR in 1937, his assessment of the company's locomotive stock was that although the existing Lord Nelson and King Arthur classes, with heavier trains and more speed a new type of engine was needed. He was given permission to build this 'mixed-traffic' engine with its distinctive casing. To retain secrecy in the railway fraternity they were built at Brighton, Eastleigh and Ashford works, this one saw service from 1941. Due to problems in clearing smoke and steam it has a different front end than when outshopped. (R.K. Blencowe Negative Archive)

RIVALRY IN THE HIGH SPEED ERA OF THE 1930s

First to Cornwall. Not only in speed but time of departure. The company started this refurbished train in 1935 with special coaches to celebrate the company's centenary at 10.30 am. 'The Limited' with its most powerful locomotives, King Class it capitalised upon its rival's problems and ran non-stop (if one ignores the stop at Newton Abbot for extra motive power to overcome the gradients to Plymouth) to Truro. However, with the King Class engines too heavy to cross the bridge into Cornwall it stopped outside Plymouth to change to a Castle Class locomotive for its journey into the Dutchy. Like the ACE, the train consisted of several portions and used the ingenious device of slipping coaches when passing some stations. They would be collected by another engine and taken to the destination all without the main train having to stop. Following a competition in *The Railway Magazine* in 1903 names for this train were invited. The general manager of the GWR chose the name, Riviera Express, although I doubt if it ever carried it. It became known as the 'Cornish Riviera Express' and to staff as 'the Limited'. To speed up services, the company used some of the money that the government made available in the 1930s to bypass Westbury and Frome. This was vital in the competition for traffic to the south-west as evidenced by the enormous load, thirteen coaches, that needed the company's largest and most powerful engines to haul. King Class engine No. 6020 *King Henry IV*, heads the 'Cornish Rivera Express' towards London in 1936, some of it is the centenary stock. Note this is a poster used to advertise the services, in the USA. (BPC)

CHAPTER 17
ENGINES TOURING ABROAD

Earlier experiences

It would always be an expensive operation to take an engine to the USA and not surprisingly, most of the Big Four were not interested. Yes, there would be publicity there, but whether it could be translated into economic interest here was another matter. The GWR had dabbled in sending an engine abroad soon after the Grouping.

London, Midland and Scottish Railway (LMSR) Experiences

The LMSR enthusiastically entered into this high cost-high publicity idea, twice. Never one to be out done, the company was not content with a mere engine as the GWR had done, but on both occasions sent a complete train, and crew to the USA. In 1933, as part of the Century of Progress Exposition, they sent one of their new Royal Scot engines

The Federal Building and the Court of the States. Appear here from the north side of the Sky Ride. (Both BPC)

In Chicago. For the 1934 festival also known as the Chicago World's Fair, held in the city of Chicago, Illinois, from 1933 to 1934, the LMSR selected one of their successful Royal Scot engines, which had been introduced in 1927. Illustrating the class is No. 6136 *The Border Regiment* at Lichfield heading towards London with the Royal Scot train in 1928. (Gordon Coltas)

In New York. The initial batch of the Coronation Class engines was so successful that another twenty were built at the Derby workshops in 1930. It is easy to see why this class of engine was selected for the 1939 New York's World Fair; gleaming, fresh from construction at nearby Crewe Works is No. 6226 *Duchess of Norfolk*. (E.R. Morten)

while for the 1939 New York World's Fair they selected a Coronation Scot engine. Discussions followed between the LMSR chairman, Sir J. Stamp, and Rufus Dawes, Chairman of the Exposition, to exhibit a whole train to tour the USA and Canada.

However, not everything was as it seemed, for both tours. For publicity purposes, the LMSR and their American hosts wanted the engine to be the first of its class. In spite of the desire, this did not happen. It was intended to exhibit No. 6100, but actually No. 6152 was used, after its number had been swapped. So the description in the brochure, 'the precursor of the class of 70 engines…' was not strictly accurate. In the later tour, there was some swapping over of numbers and names so that they matched the title of the exhibit; 'Coronation (which actually happened two years earlier in 1937) Scot' was numbered 6220. Actually No. 6229 *Duchess of Hamilton* exchanged items and went instead.

Both trains were given rapturous welcomes in the USA and to comply with safety regulations the engine was fitted with a bell and a headlight. The Royal Scot journeyed to New York and continuing to Chicago the train arrived at the exposition. Needless to say, it was roaring success with over 1 million visitors, the lucky millionth person being gifted an autographed painting. It is quite prophetic that during parts of its tour the engine had to slow down as there were so many people gathering to watch from the lineside that the authorities feared for their safety. Fast forward to today and the herald of a steam engine causes throngs of spectators – modern day trainspotters with electronic paraphernalia – to congregate at specific spots necessitating warning notices to be displayed warning the risks of trespass.

Shipping the Royal Scot. The engine was dismantled into three sections and along with eight coaches they were dispatched from Tilbury in April 1933 along with driver and fireman and other LMSR personnel. The boiler and main frame were separated and loaded onto the boat at Tilbury. After a fourteen day voyage, the engine was re-built, tested and on 1 May exhibited in Montreal. After a rapturous reception, the train crossed into the USA; the pouring rain nor the timing – midnight – did not curb the people's enthusiasm to see something English. (BPC)

Shipping the Coronation engine. This engine was dismantled differently. Here it is being lowered into the hold of the steamship *Belpamela* at Southampton. (BPC)

CHAPTER 18
CAMPING COACHES

The LNER probably had the distinction of being the first of the Big Four railway companies to offer holidays in ex-railway coaches in the early 1930s. The other companies were quick to follow suit so that at the start of the 1935 season there were around 162 sites offering 215 coaches. Within a few years this figure had mushroomed to 439 coaches, only for hostilities to curtail their growth.

LNER poster. While the thought of sleeping adjacent to a busy railway line is not to everyone's liking, to some having main line express trains a few feet from their windows was heaven indeed. (BPC)

At Dawlish Warren. Singularly or in multiples, suitable coaches were shunted into an appropriate siding where a family could enjoy a different experience than in a boarding house or a stay with relatives. Of course, they would travel to the site by rail. This modern picture is at Dawlish Warren where the ex-goods yard has been enlarged to accommodate GWR coaches. The sea is behind the photographers' position. (BPC)

Amberley. This station is on the SR line to the South Coast from Horsham, rural idyl for a peaceful holiday, complete with rabbits. (BPC)

CHAPTER 19
EXCURSIONS AND HOLIDAYS IN THE 1920s AND 1930s

While crowds flocked to see the opening of the country's first passenger carrying railway – the Liverpool to Manchester railway – in 1828, the directors knew that the real money was with goods traffic. As events transpired, for over 125 years that maxim was correct. It was only the rise of car, motorways and cheap foreign holidays that punctured this notion. The promoters of viewing the opening spectacle cashed in by conveying people to witness history. They expected it to be a one-off event and after the dust had settled, expected to go back to their money generating enterprise of transporting goods. Small wonder that people, not even passengers, were moved in goods wagons. Why would goods carrying wagons be converted for people, after all, was it not a momentary fad, soon to fade away? (All following pictures in this chapter are courtesy of BPC unless otherwise stated.)

At that time, people's only respite from the long hours at dangerous work was Sundays, and then there were other demands on their time, let alone shortage of money. Trips to the seaside and tourist attractions represented escapism for the masses. However, this pattern belies the use of Sundays. Yes, it was a day free from the grind of the factory, but it had elements of leisure incorporated into its fabric.

In the UK we owe our statutory bank holidays to John Lubbock, first Baron of Avebury, who, in 1871, drafted the Bank Holiday Bill which, when it became law, created the first bank holidays. It needs to be remembered that at that time 75–80 per cent of the population were manual workers so it made sense for employers to close their premises for a fixed period each year for maintenance purposes and as an inducement to attract and retain the best staff. Often these days coincided with traditional fairs.

Not all day-trippers went to the seaside, many preferring to go to inland attractions. Often local clubs and pubs organised trips as well as temperance societies. Trips were organised for fishing and to flower shows. This was a time to dress up in best clothes as there was bound to be 'promenading'. One of the highlights, weather permitting, of a day out at the seaside was a boat trip around the bay.

The notion that the railways 'made' the seaside towns is largely a myth. They brought unimaginable crowds to the coastal towns; however, they had already developed the habit of travelling there, well before the railways; they just made it quicker, easier and cheaper for ordinary folks to enjoy their day off. Of course there were other days off, Christmas, Easter and Whitsuntide, and for rich people, it was not the time but the place that mattered. Visits to spa towns were popular as were visits to the seaside as bathing in sea water was deemed good for one's health. Seaside resorts like Brighton, Worthing, Margate and Eastbourne boomed. Richard Hotham deliberately created a new seaside resort at Bognor Regis.

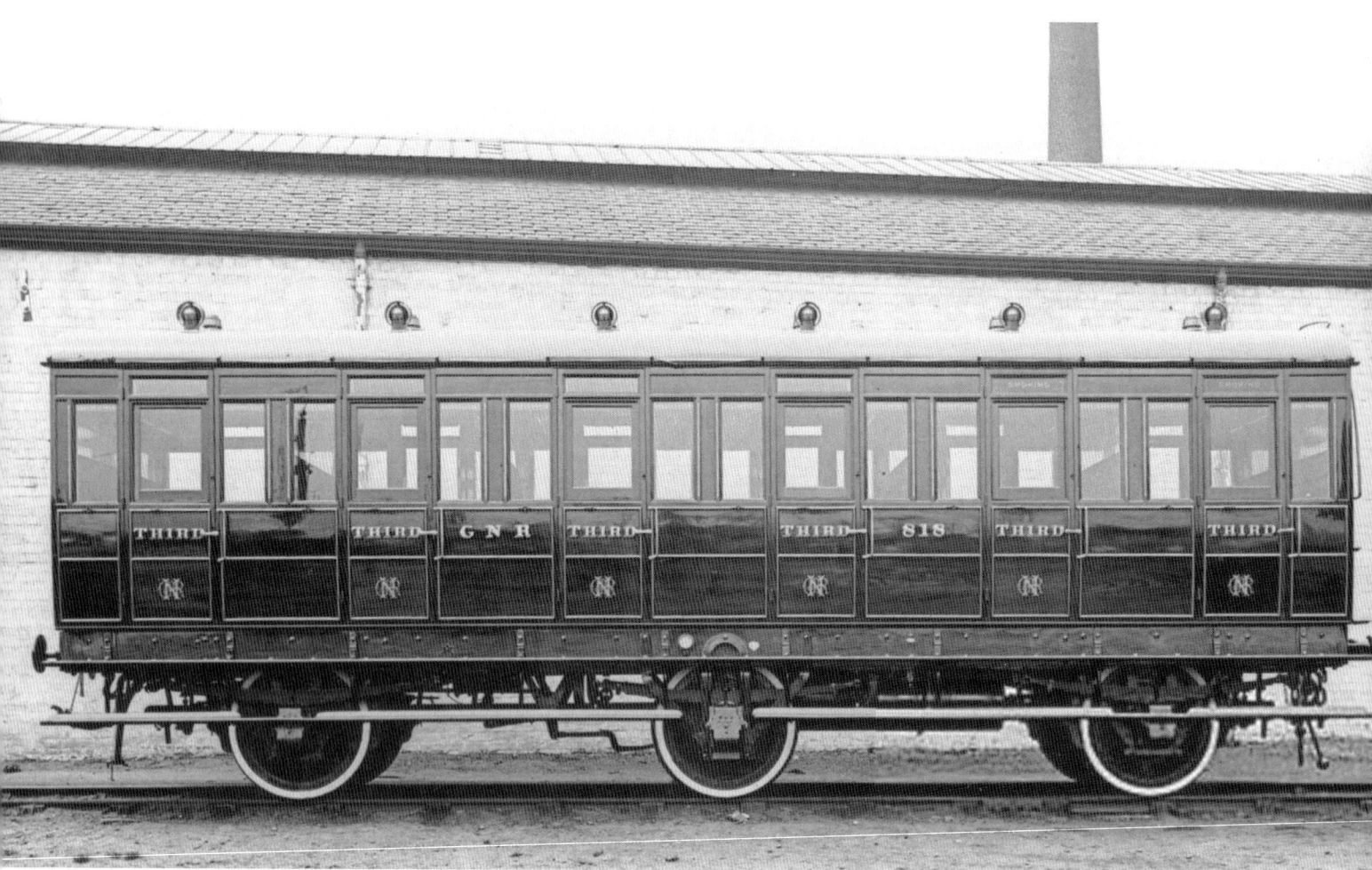

Crammed in. Carriages like this GNR six-wheeler unit made up the first 'monster' train in August 1840. Organised by Leeds Mechanics' Institute (LMI) for a trip to Hull it had 40 such carriages carrying 1,250 passengers. We are not talking about single trains but many such descending upon a destination – no wonder the residents feared the large feudal orgies with serious excesses. It was not only to seaside venues that, could be argued, organised themselves to cope such hordes, but idyllic countryside destinations like those from the mines trips arrived. For example, Wentworth Park in South Yorkshire had five trains arriving to have their day in the country. (BPC)

The following account refers to a genteel resort on the Bristol Channel and it is the words and language that the locals used when referring to visitors:

A horde of savages … a mass of boys and girls and young men and women, comprising the lowest dregs of the more disreputable neighbourhoods (of Bristol) who swarmed every avenue and invaded every nook: the songs of birds were hushed by the oaths of blasphemy, the ears of innocence shocked by the accents of obscenity, the air was polluted with the smoke of noxious pipes, gardens were robbed: drunken boys were seen staggering through every thoroughfare, fights were a frequent occurrence and scenes of lewdness met the eye. With only two policemen, aided by three special constables order could not be expected to be maintained.

Once the Bank Holiday Act was on the statute books and banks could close, staff were able to have fixed holidays, other employees had more informal arrangements

Eastborne pier. Trips around the bay. Of course, no trip to the coast would be complete without a boat trip – weather permitting. Many resorts offered not only trips around the bay but also return trips to other resorts. Piers were used, as well as beach steps, as a means of getting onto boats. (BPC)

with their employers and took their holidays to fit around the business and trade. The first bank holidays were Easter Monday, Whit Monday, the first Monday in August and Boxing Day. Confusingly, there were also public holidays, which are common law holidays that came about through habit and custom, these were Christmas Day and Good Friday. Today, the terms public and bank holiday have become interchangeable. Such days gave the impetus for promoters to put on events like race meetings and fairs, which the railway companies took advantage of by providing special trains. Regular holidays did not become a right enshrined by law until 1938. Only after that time was the majority of the working (male) population able to go away from work for more than a couple of days. Until then Sundays and a bank holiday were as good as it got. In 1937, Blackpool had 7 million overnight visitors.

Inland Attractions

Of course it was not only the seaside to which people flocked. Special events, wherever they took place, seemed to attract hordes of people with excursion trains a spectacle to be observed. Sporting fixtures always attracted vast numbers of people and racing tracks often had their own, or enlarged an ordinary, stations.

Lake Windemere. With plenty of pleasure boats to take people from the railway station around the lake and back in time for tea. Rambling was a popular pastime with many excursions to the Peak District, the canal towpaths made easy walking. The Lake District (although most are meres) has always been and continues to be a great pull for visitors, second only to Cornwall in terms of visitor numbers. (BPC)

In the East Midlands, centred around Edwinstowe are a number of large stately homes earning the line from Chesterfield to Lincoln Lancashire, Derbyshire and East Coast Railway (LD&ECR) the sobriquet, 'The Dukeries'.

Edwinstowe station. These are the refreshment rooms at Edwinstowe station, together with Langwith Junction they were the only stations along the line to boast such a facility. This train, hauled by K3 Class engine No. 61826, is returning day trippers from the Lincoln area to Nottingham district. Trips into Sherwood Forest were conducted from here also. Continuing east along this line, originally built for the movement of coal but useful for visitors, and the cathedral city of Lincoln is reached. (J.S. Gilks)

EXCURSIONS AND HOLIDAYS IN THE 1920s AND 1930s • 113

Castle Gate. It was not only the cathedral at Lincoln that drew visitors. With a castle and waterways there was plenty to see in the city. (BPC)

Promenade, Southport. No matter which station visitors arrived in to, they were well placed to take advantage of the amenities. Between the town's stations and the seafront is a wide promenade and roadway. As well as the posh shops on Lord Street and the extensive flower beds, the town also boasted the second longest pier in the country, second to Southend. (BPC)

Belle Vue, Manchester. Normally this is a two platform suburban station on the line to Marple and the Peak District. However, at weekends, holidays and for special events such as speedway, or just to visit the 'Pleasure Gardens', the services overran the platform space. As can be seen, there are also up/down bay platforms – always useful for storing coaches in. With its connections to the rail system it was well placed to send trains across to Yorkshire from either direction. With adjacent stations at Hyde Road and Longsight there was no space nor need, for extra platforms here. The travelling public had to remember which station they travelled to. (BPC)

Beaches on your doorstep

Some large centres of population are fortunate to have beaches adjacent. This enables locals to walk to the seaside with the railway companies providing transport for those a short distance away.

Sartorial elegance. Englishmen at their height. A typical working-class man has made a concession to the hot weather by wearing a short-sleeved shirt and no tie. 'Going for a dip' involved rolling up his trousers and allowing his toes to enter the water. (BPC)

Tyneside resorts

The large population in the North East have a number of nearby resorts to flock to on sunny days. I have chosen a few. Those north of the river had their railway line electrified from 1904, a typical 2-car unit having 128 seats. On holidays in the summer these would be strengthened to 4 cars, every 15 to 20 minutes, potentially 1,000 people per hour.

Right: **South Shields.** South of the Tyne estuary was an expanse of sand that every sunny day was colonised by locals. While the crowds may arrive in their own way, when it was time to go home, how many coaches would it take to transport those on the beach? (BPC)

Below: **New Brighton.** Although not jutting out into the River Mersey far, the pier boasted a salon, refreshment rooms, shelters (always useful in the English climate) and orchestra and a tower for observing ships on the opposite bank in Liverpool. At the far end was a landing stage with a ferry in attendance. Most of the people seen are likely to be from the Wirral although it was probably quicker, and cheaper, to ferry across the river to this beach than to go by train to Southport. People living along the peninsula could have arrived by electric train at the town's four platform terminus. (BPC)

Extra sidings

As can be imagined, accommodating the thousands of extra passengers for a short period of time meant that the railway companies had to have operating space so that they can detrain and somewhere for the carriages to be stored, especially during the winter.

Southport, 1939. Looking west from the footbridge shows the arrangement at Chapel Street station in all its splendour. While the main purpose of the picture is to show this one coach train, probably destined for the line to Barton, it usefully shows the extra platforms, on the right. This very wide platform, 'London Street excursion platform' had its own access. On the right are extensive carriage sidings. (Milepost 92½ Picture Library)

Southport poster. Thousands flocked to the sands, pier and attractions of the town every year. Inaugurated in 1924 was an annual flower show. A railway sponsored office was to guide people during the show. With both LNER and LMSR having a presence in the town then it was important that passengers remembered your brand. (BPC)

Lord Street station. Although there was little room to enlarge Chapel Street station, the town was blessed with more platform space, actually nearer the attractions. A train has just arrived at the recently – two years ago – extended platform at Cheshire Lines Railway's Lord Street station, in 1951. On the left is some point-work showing how the engines were released having arrived with coaches. Due to a triangular arrangement of lines near Hunt's Cross, trains from both Liverpool and Manchester could access the station. Although other lines meant a shorter journey time, these four extra platforms were welcome. (This would be the station's summer finale, closing the next January.) (J. Peden)

Great Western Railway (GWR)

Weston-super-Mare

There were also steam excursions to Wales, which although choppy and windy, were very popular on both sides of the Channel. Steamers from Wales brought an increase in income prompting the further development with refreshment rooms, a concert hall, reading rooms, an extended pavilion, a lifeboat station and a low-water jetty over the next twenty years. However, on Boxing Day 1897, most of the structures on the island were destroyed by fire – replacements were completed just eight months later. A new pier – the more central Grand Pier – opened for business in 1904. Five years later, the southern end of the island was increased by over half an acre by the construction of a concrete platform. This new area housed a roller-skating rink, a bioscope theatre,

Overflow platforms. The town's rise to prominence is due to its extensive safe bathing beeches and its spring water arising from the nearby Mendip Hills. The main through platforms here are on a tight curve, opened in 1884, and so to cope with excursion traffic the GWR built a set of platforms adjacent to their main station, which they renamed, General. The four terminal platforms accessed onto Locking Road, the station taking that name, opening in 1914. (BPC)

Pier. Apart from the open space, the tide goes along way out in the Bristol Channel, there is a small outcrop of rock to the north, a little way from the shore. A pier was built from the shore to Birnbeck Rock, opening in 1864; it saw 120,000 visitors in the first three months, making it quite a successful venture. (BPC)

Weston-super-Mare's other railway. A coastal light railway line, around 12 miles long connected Portishead to Clevedon to Weston-super-Mare, opening in 1897. The line boasted it was the 'shortest and quickest route between Weston, Clevedon and Portishead'. This is the southern end with a terminus station at Ashcombe Road, a short walk from the beach. Although closure was two years away, as can be seen it still conveyed a fair number of passengers. Not surprising as the main line was somewhat inland and the settlements were along the coast, served by this light railway. (BPC)

a flying machine, switchback railway and the famous water chute ride. This effort to attract customers from its newer rival was successful and throughout the 1920s and early 1930s, the old pier was the number one destination for both visitors and residents alike. However, the Grand Pier fought back by opening a funfair of its own, a decision from which Birnbeck never recovered. In 1941, the pier was taken over by the Admiralty and closed to the public – with the fairground and all amusement rides dismantled and removed – before being commissioned as HMS *Birnbeck*, a secret facility for weapons testing. Serious damage was caused to the island when a Wellington bomber, operating out of nearby RAF Locking, inadvertently released a dummy mine whilst flying overhead. When hostilities were over, the pier was handed back to its rightful owners and, whilst the steamer service was resumed, Birnbeck became a much more sedate place, with just a refreshment room and no amusements. Using the lifeboat station as an anchor, there is hope that the pier will re-invent itself as a tourist attraction.

Blackpool

This must be the ultimate in seaside resorts on the West Coast. It is hard for us today to appreciate the sheer number of visitors arriving in Blackpool on bank holidays around eighty years ago. It coped with the vast number of visitors by having two stations; one, Central, boasting at its furthest extent, fourteen platforms.

Not only was Blackpool by the sea, it also had an extensive funfair, piers and gardens for promenading along its Golden Mile. People on day trips put on their 'Sunday best' to impress. The town boasted a sea front tram, its own unique 'city tour'.

Talbot Road station. The other main line station, Talbot Road, consisted of two parallel train sheds. Platforms 1 to 6 were located in the sheds, with a larger island between platforms 1 and 2 to accommodate taxis. In addition, there was effectively, in all but name, a separate station at the east end of Queen Street, with open 'excursion' platforms 7 to 16, used only in summer. (BPC)

'The Yorkshire Riviera'

The East Coast had many towns such as Whitby, Staithes, Saltburn, Scarborough, Filey, Hornsea, Bridlington and others, which all tried to entice visitors.

Bridlington. After the First World War, excursion platforms were added to cope with the many special trains. On summer Saturdays the timetable would include through trains to Leeds, London, the Midlands and Derbyshire. This post-war picture shows the 10.00 am Leeds to Bridlington express behind B1 Class No. 61065. The inter-war period saw the greatest extent of the station complete with engine shed and two turntables with extensive sidings. (B.K.B. Green)

'Queen of Yorkshire'

Scarborough vied for this accolade.

Named train. To give some impression of how important the town was to the railway company, the LNER, a special train, Scarborough Flyer, was introduced in 1923, officially named in 1927. Behind A3 Pacifics the train was one of the fastest runs from King's Cross to York as seen here with No. 4480 *Enterprise* in charge. There, a portion for Whitby was detached. So popular was this train, in summer months only restaurant train that on Saturdays extra trains to the two resorts of Scarborough and Whitby were operated. (RAS)

Steam railcar. At one time, in the 1930s, the town had no less than five funicular railways, adding to its charm. These helped people descend the steep cliffs from their hotels to the seaside. In one of the shorter platforms, awaiting its next turn is one of the company's steam railcars, No. 246 *Royal Sovereign*.
(Roger Carpenter)

The rise of the holiday camp

Skegness

GNR poster. In 1908 the famous 'Jolly Fisherman' poster was used by GNR to advertise day trips from King's Cross in London. By 1913, more than 750,000 people made excursions to the town. (BPC)

Above: **Firsby.** Lincolnshire is a predominantly an agricultural county with few centres of any sizeable population. The first railway line from Grimsby to Boston was several miles inland passing through Louth and Firsby. When visiting the seaside by rail became popular in the late nineteenth century, the GNR was approached about a branch to the coast; they refused, short sightedly as events turned out. A local company built the branch from the latter to the small village of Wainfleet, later extended to Skegness in 1873. However, the junction at Firsby faced away from the most important traffic, and so a west to south curve was installed in 1881. (BPC)

Opposite above: **Skegness branch.** Looking south from the footbridge at the station shows the connection to the Skegness branch on the left. Skegness, as a seaside destination, existed before Butlin's arrived on the scene. A local landowner had seen his local rental income decline due to a trade depression in agriculture and decided that his fortunes might be revived if he turned Skegness into a seaside resort. A road plan was developed, plots of land for houses and a pier were developed as well as investing in a sewage system, a sea wall and a road direct from the train station to the sea front. Newspapers across the Midlands advertised properties, and shops began opening. Skegness had become known as a trippers' paradise' by 1880. Skegness and other 'lower' status resorts provided cheap amusements, beach entertainers, street traders and, by the end of the nineteenth century, spectacular entertainment for a mass market. Hoards would arrive in to the town's station. Its popularity as a tourist destination grew after the First World War. Billy Butlin (who had been a stall holder on the beach since 1925) built permanent amusements south of the pier in 1929. In 1932, the first illuminations were turned on and the following year Butlin launched a carnival. Cinemas and casinos joined the theatres of the Edwardian period as popular attractions, while some of the apartments and houses by the seafront were converted into shops, cafés and arcades. However, the pattern and desires of visitors was changing. In 1936, Butlin built his own all-in holiday camp in Ingoldmells, providing constant entertainment and facilities for guests. It was joined in 1939 by the Derbyshire Miners' Holiday Camp. (BPC)

Opposite below: **Eastern Belle.** Hauled by No. 8790 this was an interesting train, introduced in 1929. Its seven Pullman coaches departed from Liverpool Street station in London to a variety of resorts, depending on which day of the week. Here it is ready to depart for the return trip from Skegness (often referred to as 'Nottingham by the sea'); other venues included Cromer (pier available), Sheringham, Lowestoft and Hunstanon. (BPC)

EXCURSIONS AND HOLIDAYS IN THE 1920s AND 1930s • 127

Butlin's

Butlin's first holiday camp was a phenomenal success, attracting some 10,000 enquiries from the initial half-page advertisement placed in the *Daily Express*, promising 'holidays with three meals a day and free entertainment from 35s per week according to season'. The idea was so popular with the public that by the time the camp first opened its doors on Easter Saturday in 1936, it was already fully booked for the season. Butlin's original idea came from dissatisfaction with the traditional boarding house accommodation that he had stayed in during his former career as a travelling showman. 'I felt sorry for myself, but I felt even sorrier for the families with young children as they trudged along wet and bedraggled, or forlornly filled in time in amusement arcades until they could return to the boarding houses.'

The Butlin's Camp was a miniature seaside resort, only more so. It sought to create a fantasy world for its residents within its perimeters. That fantasy world was the one they had seen at the cinema and read about in popular magazines such as *Picture Goer*, which talked at length about the extravagant lifestyles of the movie stars among numerous glossy pictures. What Butlin attempted to do was to allow his campers the opportunity to escape from their daily lives, not for a couple of hours at the cinemas, but for a whole week.

In advertising the camps, Butlin teamed up with the LNER, who had an interest in promoting holidays on the East Coast. LNER actually paid for 50 per cent of all Butlin's advertising costs and Butlin's second camp at Clacton was opened on an LNER line. The Clacton Camp is illustrated by a delightful railway poster produced by LNER showing the swimming pool in the foreground and the main camp building bearing Butlin's famous motto: 'Our true intent is all for your delight.' Although this is a quote from Shakespeare, Butlin confessed he borrowed it from a fairground organ in *The Billy*

Butlin's. This aerial view shows the proximity of the camp to the sea. (BPC)

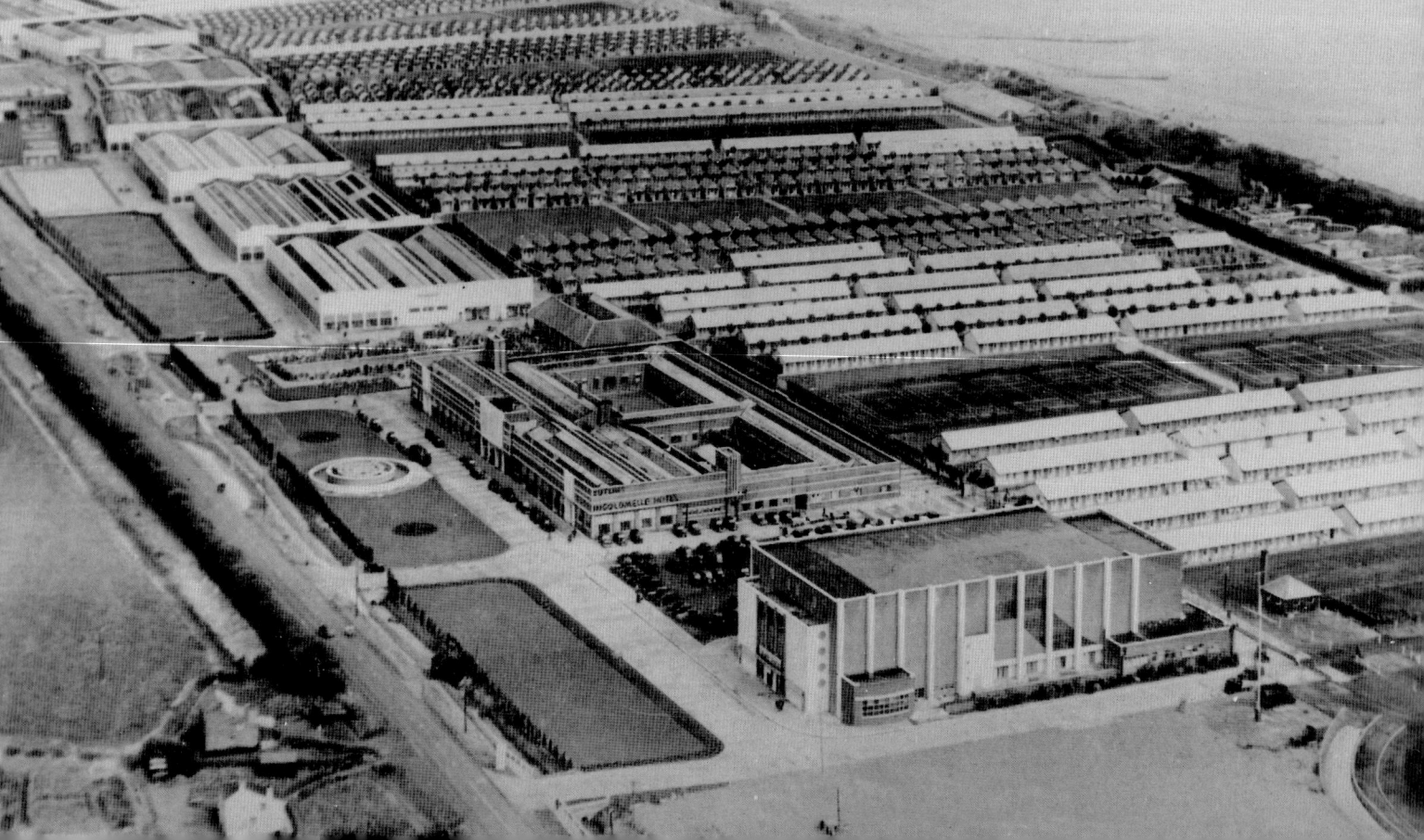

BUTLIN'S SKEGNESS
The Boating Lake

Iconic uniform. In addition to the major stars from the early days, the Butlin's Red Coats were always on hand to ensure that the campers got the most from their holidays. The idea for the Red Coats came to Butlin early on in the Skegness camp's first season. He saw the first campers walking around looking bored and not making full use of the facilities. They had come to the camp looking for companionship and were not finding it. One of his assistants, Norman Bradford, started to 'jolly up' proceedings by telling a few jokes to the campers assembled in the dining room. Butlin thought this was a good idea and the next day asked his colleague to go out and buy a distinctively coloured blazer – he did, in blue, primrose yellow and white, the camp colours. Butlin was not convinced and asked him instead to buy a red blazer. The Red Coats were then born. The famous 'Hi-De-Hi, Ho-De-Ho' routine also started in the 1930s – Butlin borrowed the idea from an army routine in an American film – continuing the cinema link. (BPC)

Butlin Story. This type of poster would have been seen in LNER trains and stations in the late 1930s. Since train travel had only the motor bus to compete with for the majority of holidaymakers, this was a sure way of attracting customers to LNER. The popularity of the camps increased further when the government passed legislation giving all industrial workers a week's paid holiday in 1938. Butlin's advertisements proclaimed; 'Holidays with pay: Holidays with play: A week's holiday for a week's wage'. By the end of the 1930s, fifteen million people had paid holidays. However, in spite of this campaign, the majority of Butlin's campers were not drawn from the working classes, but were from the lower-middle classes, often bank clerks and their wives. The cost of even catering on a mass scale was still too high for most working people, who still tended to go to the traditional boarding houses. The Second World War came as a shock to Billy Butlin in 1939; he had confidently predicted that the crisis would blow over and was already planning his next camp at Filey, on the East Coast, due to open in 1940. However, in true entrepreneurial style, he coped with the war when it came. Through a deal with the war ministry, who took over his camps at Clacton and Skegness, he completed the camp at Filey and built two other camps at Ayr and Pwllheli. He negotiated a scheme giving him the right to buy the camps back at the end of the war and at the close of hostilities, Butlin was left in a very strong position. His camps really came into their own in the 1950s and became the epitome of the working man's holiday in that era. The pioneer camps fared less well and many never re-opened. For some, the true spirit of camp life was lost forever.

Seaton Junction station. The connection here, initially named Colyton Junction, changed its name to Seaton Junction in 1869. The branch was on the down side with the main road access being to the up side, with a footbridge connecting the two main platforms. A footpath went straight across the main lines from Shute Road to south of the branch line. In 1927/28, the section of line through the station was enlarged. The main buildings, and the goods shed, on the up side, to the right, remained, while a new layout incorporating up/down platform loops was built. The original footbridge was lengthened so that it spanned all four lines, and a new set of down-side buildings was built on the new down platform, on the left. A very long concrete variety was built to carry the footpath across the four running lines, almost obscured by the platform footbridge. (BPC)

Transport by train. Having passed through Prestatyn station, this train was the Holyhead-bound Crab Class engine No. 2841 passing a fine example of a signal bridge for down trains. Such was the volume of traffic to the vitally important port of Holyhead that there were two tracks in each direction, the train is on the down fast line. Curiously as it seems, there are three signals facing us. The far left is for the slow line, the arm on the taller post is for the fast line and the middle post is used to indicate trains transferring from the fast to slow lines, usually if the train is to stop at the station. This large seafront camp was officially opened on 24 June 1939, by Lord Stamp, chairman of the LMSR, illustrating the joint venture nature of the camp. (E.R. Morten)

In the late 1930s a joint LMSR-Thomas Cook venture saw the opening of a camp on the North Wales coast at Prestatyn. Calling itself the 'Chalet Village by the sea', or 'Cook's Camp', it could cater for up to 1,750 people. Unlike its competitors, this camp was meant to be an 'up market, last word in luxurious, chalet by the sea'. Close by was Llandudno, styling itself as, 'Queen of the Welsh Resorts'.

CHAPTER 20
NAMED TRAINS IN THE POST-GROUPING YEARS

All of the Big Four were publicity conscious and sought new ways to entice the public to their services. Generally they were not in competition, running to different towns and cities, but were keen to develop brand awareness so that a passenger would automatically look to their services rather than a rival's. To this end, they all wanted eye-catching names for certain express trains, some of which are represented below.

Great Western Railway (GWR)

Cheltenham Spa Express. By the early 1930s, due to the use of Castle Class engines, this train, also known as the Cheltenham Flyer, was laying claim to be 'the fastest train in the world', covering the journey from Paddington to Swindon at an average speed of 70mph. In those publicity conscious times, this was front page news. Charging through Iver, near Slough, was engine No. 5094 *Tretower Castle*. The use of reporting numbers on the front of trains was a practice the GWR introduced from 1934.

Fierce rivalry between the four main railway companies during the 1920s and 1930s to run the fastest train in the country, and therefore in the world, led to accelerations to the service. In July 1929 the scheduled journey time became seventy minutes, an average speed of 66.2mph, and publicity proclaimed this as 'the fastest train in the world'. By now the train had acquired its popular nickname of the Cheltenham Flyer, although this was never adopted officially. Two years later in 1931 the accolade was claimed by the Canadian Pacific Railroad as they ran a train with a slightly faster schedule, taking the 'fastest train in the world' title. The GWR train was again accelerated in July to an average speed of 69.2mph. On Monday, 6 June 1932, the train broke railway speed records with a time of fifty-six minutes and forty-seven seconds at an average speed of 81.6mph. Such a journey speed had never been previously recorded and this made its run the fastest railway run in the world. The train was hauled by Castle Class No. 5006 *Tregenna Castle*. In September 1932, the time from Swindon to London was further reduced to sixty-five minutes, giving an extraordinary average speed, for the time, of 71.3mph over the whole trip of 77¼ miles. This was the first occasion in the history of railways that any train had been scheduled at over 70mph. (SLS)

Southern Railway (SR)

The pre-Grouping company, the LB&SCR began using Pullman cars in its express trains in 1875, and in December 1881 they introduced the first all-Pullman train in the UK. Known as the 'Pullman Limited', this ran between London Victoria and Brighton. In 1888, a second all-Pullman service was instituted, using cars lit by electricity.

Left: **Golden Arrow.** This must be one of the country's most famous trains. It scored over its rivals by being all-Pullman coaches and extending the service to Paris with all the glamour of the 1920s and 1930s. This poster shows engine No. 853 *Sir Richard Greville*. All the Big Four produced pictures made into wooden jigsaws, now valuable collectors' pieces. The *Flèche d'Or* was introduced in 1926 as an all first class Pullman service between Paris and Calais. On 15 May 1929, the SR introduced the equivalent between London Victoria and Dover while simultaneously launching a new first class only ship, the *Canterbury*, for the ferry crossing. The train usually consisted of ten cars, hauled by one of the SR's most powerful engines, and took ninety-eight minutes to travel between London and Dover. Because of the impact of air travel and 'market forces' on the underlying economy of the service, ordinary first- and third-class carriages were added in 1931. Similarly, the first class-only ferry, *Canterbury*, was modified to allow other classes of passengers. (BPC)

Below: **Brighton Belle.** Before the line from London to Brighton was completely electrified in 1933, the steam hauled Southern Belle train plied the line. Its replacement took the form of a five coach, all-Pullman set, claiming to take one hour for the journey. This is one of the three new sets for the service there being three up and three down trains per day. Its posters emphasised 'electric', 'one hour' and 'Pullman' to entice passengers. (BPC)

The LB&SCR was the origin of the British umber and cream Pullman livery and in 1906 this colour scheme was also adopted by the Pullman Company, with the name of the car in large gilt letters on the lower panel and flanked on each side by a coloured transfer of the Pullman Company's crest.

Another all-Pullman service was introduced in 1908 under the name of the Southern Belle. Contemporary advertising by the LB&SCR claimed that this was 'the most luxurious train in the world'. In 1908, this could be experienced for a special London Victoria to Brighton day return fare of 12 shillings, a premium rate at a time when average earnings were around £1 a week. The Southern Belle was steam hauled until 1 January 1933, when electric units were introduced. Trial trains had commenced running between London and Brighton on 2 November 1932, using an experimental five-coach unit (No. 2001) and examples of the new rolling stock were exhibited at London Victoria and Brighton stations from 29 December 1932. With the arrival of the mid day Victoria to Brighton service at Brighton station on 29 June 1934, the mayor of Brighton renamed the train the Brighton Belle, and it retained this title until withdrawal. The service was scheduled to take sixty minutes for the 51-mile express journey. Three five-car all-Pullman electric multiple units (EMUs) designated were commissioned by the SR as the flagship of the world's then largest electrification project, which covered over 160 miles of track. The fifteen cars – built in 1932 by the Metropolitan Cammell Carriage and Wagon Company (MCCW) – later know as the Metro-Cammell – at its Saltley Works in Birmingham – were operated in trains comprising two units, the remaining unit normally held in reserve.

London, Midland and Scottish Railway (LMSR)

Two named trains went from St Pancras to Scotland, daily. The original name The Waverley was given to the morning departure from London by the LMSR in September 1927. Its sister train to Glasgow, which departed an hour later, was named the Thames-Clyde Express. They were not particularly fast but excelled in connectivity. Both trains were products of a publicity drive by the MR from 1927. Both traversed England, serving the industrial heart of Yorkshire (Sheffield and Leeds) and passing through the scenic Settle and Carlisle line. There they diverged. The train to Waverley station in Scotland's capital using the aptly named Waverley route whilst the train for Glasgow's St Enoch's station went via Dumfries. Both entailed a change of engines at Leeds city station, which in later days involved 'Royal Scot' and 'A3' class engines, it used the Settle and Carlisle line. Here is, for some reason the re-named the *Thames-Forth Express*, which is hauled by No. 5568 *Western Australia*. Note the owner's initials on the tender. With their very similar routes and timings, the train to Edinburgh was regarded in some circles as a relief for the Glasgow train as far as Carlisle. (BPC)

They could not compete for the London to Scotland traffic with the faster trains travelling on the West Coast and East Coast. They travelled by the former MR's main line through Leicester, sometimes with reversals when serving Derby and Nottingham, as far as Leeds. After another reversal there, the train crossed the Pennines to the scenic route, still on former MR territory. Its route was longer and steeper, and MR expresses could not ignore major population centres en route, especially Leicester, Sheffield and Leeds.

In Scotland, it took a longer route in order to provide a service to Dumfries, Kilmarnock and finally, Glasgow St Enoch, the city's G&SWR terminus.

London and North Eastern Railway (LNER)

The origins of this train stem from pre-Grouping times. The first Special Scotch Express ran in 1862, with simultaneous departures at 10.00 am from the GNR's King's Cross and the North British Railway's (NBR) Edinburgh Waverley. The original journey took 10½ hours, including a half an hour stop at York for lunch. Increasing competition and improvements in railway technology saw this time reduced to 8½ hours by 1888. From 1896, the train was modernised, introducing such features as corridors between carriages, heating and dining cars. As passengers could now take luncheon on the train, the York stop was reduced to fifteen minutes, but the end to end journey time remained 8½ hours. Like the earlier carriages built for the service, this rolling stock was jointly owned by the three operating companies and formed part of the pool known as the East Coast Joint Stock (ECJS). With the advent of the Grouping and both companies becoming part of the LNER and it was re-named, Flying Scotsman from 1924, although

Flying Scotsman. Arguably the most famous train in the world. Emerging in 1924 from the Special Scotch Express this non-stop restaurant express train appeared in 1928. Here A3 Class engine, also called *Flying Scotsman* is in charge of the 10.00 am departure from King's Cross on its 400 mile race to Edinburgh. (RAS)

this was the commonly used title for the train since inception. To further publicise the train, a recently built A1 Class locomotive numbered 1472 and, subsequently, No. 4472 was named after the service and put on display at the 1924 British Empire Exhibition, seen earlier.

Due to a long-standing agreement between the competing coastal companies since the famous railway races of the previous century, speeds of the Scotch expresses were limited, the time for the 392 miles between the capitals to a pedestrian 8 hours 15 minutes. However, following experimentation that drastically reduced the fuel consumption it was discovered that it would be possible to run the entire distance, non-stop on one tender of coal. Solving one problem resulted in another – footplate fatigue. To solve this issue, ten special corridor tenders were built with a coal capacity of 9 tons instead of the usual 8; means were also given to access the locomotive from the train through a narrow passageway inside the tender tank plus a flexible bellows connection linking it with the leading coach. The passageway, which ran along the right-hand side of the tender, imposed restrictions on the crew using it; it was 5ft high and 18in wide. The locomotive No. 4472 *Flying Scotsman* hauled the inaugural non-stop train from London on 1 May 1928, and it successfully ran the 392 miles (631km) between Edinburgh and London without stopping, a record at the time for a scheduled service. The 1928 non-stop Flying Scotsman had improved catering and other on-board services – even a barber's shop. With the end of the limited speed agreement in 1932, journey time came down to 7 hours 30 minutes, and by 1938 to 7 hours 20 minutes. As a spoiler to the LNER publicity, four days earlier, the LMSR had performed a one-off stunt by running the Edinburgh section of its Royal Scot train the 399 miles non-stop from Euston.

CHAPTER 21
1930s STORIES THAT WEREN'T HAPPY ENDINGS

Air traffic

The railway companies saw air traffic, especially on longer routes, as a threat to their railway services. Some would argue that streamlining was an attempt by the railways to combat such innovations. Consequently, they sought the Parliamentary Bill of 1929 that gave the Railway companies permission to operate their own air services within their own territory and in Europe. The Big Four and Imperial Airways operated out of the airline's base at Croydon Airport. The most important Railway Air Services (RAS) route flown was between London and Scotland (London-Birmingham-Liverpool and Liverpool-Belfast-Glasgow). The trunk service commenced on 20 August 1934 and it was mainly aimed at passengers wishing to connect at Croydon Airport with Imperial Airways' flights to the Continent, operating once daily in each direction. Other routes had started before then, by the GWR from Plymouth (stopping at Torbay) to Cardiff, from 12 April 1933.

Financially the venture was unrewarding with limited and variable traffic. In 1939, the operation of civil aircraft was restricted, and part of the RAS fleet was placed under government control. The aircraft were involved in communications flights for the military within the British Isles. By 1940, the RAF had taken over all the military communication tasks and the airline returned to flying routes 'of national importance'. In practice, wartime operations were restricted to the Liverpool-Belfast-Glasgow route carrying government and other 'priority' passengers and mail. RAS resumed peacetime flights in early 1946. However, in that summer, the government effectively nationalised the service, ceasing on 31 January 1947. Shoreham Airport (also known as Bungalow Halt), was opened in 1910, and had service to Liverpool and Manchester, and from Croydon also.

Aircraft. This is the sort of vehicle used for the service; de Havilland Dragon Rapide. (BPC)

CHAPTER 22
LINE CLOSURES BEFORE DR BEECHING

Rumour and folklore blame Dr Beeching for the closure of the nation's railway lines in the 1960s and beyond. However, uneconomic lines had always been under scrutiny. To illustrate that closure was not a new phenomenon, here are a few from after the First World War. (All pictures in this chapter are courtesy of BPC.)

The Dyke station near Brighton. Just west of Brighton but east of Hove station was a short 3.5 miles to the Devil's Dyke branch. So popular was this natural feature, it soon became a tourist landscape attraction hosting 30,000 on August bank holiday, six years after opening. Operations continued until 1917 when, in the midst of the First World War, the line was closed as a wartime economy measure, re-opening in 1920. The SR purchased a Sentinel-Cammell steam railcar in June 1933 for use on the branch. Although operationally successful, the single railcar with its forty-four seats was not large enough to meet the needs of the line at weekends. Just as the branch left the main line, it developed a timber platform, at Rowan Halt, in 1934. Being capable of carrying more passengers per day, road transport led to the line's closure in 1938.

West Bay, Bridport. Branching from the GWR's Yeovil to Dorchester line at Maiden Newton was an 11.25 mile branch to Bridport. Later the line was extended through the town to West Bay and its harbour. The passenger service using the extension led to its closure during the First World War and also during 1921 and 1924, finally ceasing in 1930. Trains continued to run, despite changes in ownership from SR to GWR, for another forty-five years. Looking away from the terminus shows the single branch heading towards the town of Bridport. (BPC)

Akeld (LNER). It was on the Alnwick to Cornhill branch which ran from Alnwick to Cornhill Junction on the Kelso line near Coldstream. The line had difficulty attracting passengers as many of the stations were some distance from the communities they served. Increased bus competition in the 1920s led to passenger trains being withdrawn on 22 September 1930. (BPC)

The line had a chequered time after nationalisation. Severe storms in 1948 washed away a bridge north of Ilderton station and such was the level of traffic that it was not deemed economic to replace it. The line was effectively split into two parts. The section to Ilderton was served by its link to Alnwick while the line to Wooler, which included Akeld, connected to Coldstream. The infrequent services along both sections caused the lines to go into further decline with the section from Alnwick to Ilderton closing on 2 March 1953 with the other section and Akeld station following suit on 29 March 1965.

Great Western Railway (GWR) Electrification

Who said, 'Never let the truth get in the way of a good story'? Never openly discussed, let alone materialised, were plans to electrify the GWR main lines west of Taunton to Exeter and onto Newton Abbot. In 1935 the price of coal increasingly concerned the GWR board, especially prices at the pithead but also the cost of moving the coal from South Wales to engine sheds. Electrification of the heavy gradients along the line west of Taunton could raise the overall speed of trains. However, the density of trains along the line, except for holiday times, would not justify the capital cost of special equipment. Consequently, these plans never saw the light of day, much to the delight of GWR steam devotees who were horror-struck at the idea of 'juice trains' west of Exeter.

CHAPTER 23
LONDON TRANSPORT BOARD

The existing Big Four railways found they were unable to cope with the expansion of housing around London following the First World War. A programme was developed under which branches of the Big Four became part of an underground system. A pooling of receipts partly compensated the railway companies for their loss of traffic and revenue. The London Passenger Transport Board (LPTB) – also shortened to London Transport (LT), as this new body was called, embarked on a massive capital investment programme that not only extended services, but also reconstructed many existing assets. This mostly came under the umbrella of the 1935-40 'New Works Programme'. This encompassed closing a handful of stations, opening new ones. Other works consisted of laying extra lines, new tunnels, installation of colour light signals, and platform extensions for stations. The programme also saw major reconstructions of many central area Underground stations, with escalators being installed to replace lifts; extensions of several Tube lines; and connection to and electrification of a number of suburban lines. It involved extensions to the Central, Bakerloo, Northern and Metropolitan lines, the provision of new trains and maintenance depots, and the extensive rebuilding of many central area stations. The board's tramways were replaced by what was to become one of the world's largest trolleybus systems. It was also during this period that two icons of London Transport were first seen – 1938 Tube stock trains and the RT-type bus. Although curtailed and delayed by the outbreak of the Second World War, the programme delivered much of the present Underground system.

London Transport was the organisation responsible for transport in London and its environs from 1933 until 1948. Its origins were odd, originated in one Parliament and continued under the following parliament of different persuasion. Given the range and scale of the works it would be impossible to go into meaningful details and so a random collection of the new works, both in picture and text, are included. The company used imaginative methods of publicity using the idea of the rings around the planet Saturn to represent their image of the Tube.

Ex-Southern Railway (SR) Lines

With little penetration of London Transport into the area of the SR, the LPTB had few examples of the improvements and transfer of services from the main to Tube systems. In some people's eyes, much of the suburban electric system of the SR should be regarded as the 'Tube in suburbia'.

New stock. Ninety-two transport and ancillary undertakings, with a capital of approximately £120 million, came under the LPTB. Central buses, trolleybuses, Underground trains and trams were painted in 'Underground' and 'London general' red, coaches and country buses in green, with coaches branded Green Line. Already in use on most of the Tube system, 'UNDERGROUND' branding was extended to all lines and stations. During this period, two icons of London Transport were first seen, 1938 Tube stock trains having earned their keep on the Isle of Wight have now been replaced, and the RT-type bus. Here at New Cross depot are some of the 1938 carriages, one aspect of the New Works Programme.

A total of 1,121 cars were built by Metro-Cammell and Birmingham Railway Carriage and Wagon Company (BRC&W). The trains represented a major technical advance, as all the electrical equipment was located under the floor for the first time. All previous Tube stock had large equipment compartments behind the driving cabs in motor cars, which reduced the space available for passengers by about a third. The trains were primarily intended for use on the Northern and Bakerloo lines, with an additional seven trains also being used on the Piccadilly line. As part of the New Works Programme, the Northern and Central lines were to be extended over LNER tracks, and because of a joint working agreement between the LPTB and the LNER, it was necessary for a proportion of the Underground fleet to be owned by the LNER. Accordingly, 289 cars of 1938 stock were designated as LNER owned and fitted with plates marked 'Property of LNER'. Although 129 of these were to cover extensions to the Central line, none of them actually worked Central line services – they were mixed with the Northern and Bakerloo line fleets.

As part of the New Works Programme, there were plans to operate nine-car trains of 1938 stock on the Northern line. These cars were originally numbered differently from the other cars, the first digit 1 being replaced by a 9. So successful was the 1938 stock that, in 1948, when additional cars were needed, ninety-one almost identical cars were built. These were known as 1949 stock and operated with the 1938 stock.

With the line ending at Finsbury Park from 1906, the GNR hoped passengers would transfer to their surface level trains. Very soon after opening it was clear that the termination of the line in urban Finsbury Park rather than further out of central London in more suburban Wood Green, Southgate or Tottenham had been a mistake. Passengers leaving the line preferred to transfer on to trams and buses for the continuation of their journeys, rather than use the GNR as it had hoped. This caused much inconvenience and congestion in and around the station at Finsbury Park. Calls for extending the line gathered strength after the First World War. In the face of mounting pressure, the LNER continued the opposition of its predecessor, the GNR, to a northward extension of the Piccadilly line although it did begin developing plans for the electrification of its own suburban services. When the LNER cancelled the electrification of its routes due to lack of money, a petition from the Middlesex Federation of Ratepayers in 1923 finally spurred the government to act and, in 1925, The North and North-East London Traffic Inquiry was set up to examine options. When the inquiry reported, it recommended an extension of initially only one station to Manor House. The LNER was placed in the position of either carrying out the electrification of its own services or withdrawing its veto to an extension of the

Cockfosters. The station opened on 31 July 1933 as the northern terminus of the line from Finsbury Park, it was suggested that its name be Cockfosters. It was designed in the European style and is now a Grade II listed building. (BPC)

Piccadilly line. To make the extension financially worthwhile, a route was proposed out to rural Oakwood and Cockfosters although the group did not actually have the money to construct even the limited extension.

The recession of the late 1920s eventually provided the economic imperative for the construction of the extension. The government introduced the Development (Loan Guarantees and Grants) Act in 1930. The aim was to increase employment through a stimulation of public works projects and, with guarantees available on the money needed for the construction, the Underground Group was able to start work on the Cockfosters extension, the Piccadilly line western extension as well as many other projects throughout the Underground network. Despite the Underground Group's wish to construct most of the extension on the surface, the first four stations are underground. The line surfaces at Arnos Grove before going back into a tunnel to pass through a hill at Southgate. North of Southgate, the line is on the surface for the rest of the route to Cockfosters. Therefore, five of the eight stations on the extension are underground.

Central line extensions

The line was extended at both ends. In the west, from North Acton to connect to and take over the GWR's suburban line to Denham and eastern extension from Liverpool Street to connect to and take over the LNER's lines to Epping and Ongar – the aim of all of us who have tried to visit all Tube stations in one day. Following the LPTB takeover, the Harry Beck-designed Tube map began to show the route's name as the Central London line instead of Central London railway. In anticipation of the extensions taking its services far beyond the boundaries of the borough of London, the word 'London' was omitted from the name on 23 August 1937; thereafter it was simply the Central line.

CHAPTER 24
NEW ENGINES BUILT DURING THE 1940s

LNER locomotive. A reader may have thought that as the late 1920s and 1930 were times of innovation and the production of bigger, more powerful locomotives then this demand, and solution, would continue during the next decade. However, there became a little matter of another world war to contend with. With passenger traffic heavily supressed and so the development of its engines to increase performance inhibited, all attention turned to maximising the performance of freight engines. Engines such as this O4 Class from the GCR were the doyen of heavy freight haulage during the First World War. Here is O4 Class No. 6229 taking empty coal wagons across the Pennines for refilling at pits in Yorkshire in 1939. Being built in 1912 it gave sterling service in the first conflict so why not again? Over 300 such GCR engines were built here and shipped abroad during the First World War – would the same happen again? (E.R. Morten)

Readers are probably aware that pictures taken during conflicts are rare and often of variable quality. I would ask them to bear this in mind, when reading this chapter especially. After the start of hostilities in 1939, most of the country's railway works went over to producing armaments. No one knew how long this was to last. On the cusp of war, the government created a new department, Ministry of Supply. Building on the experiences during the First World War, thinking was that there would be a large demand for locomotives to be sent to France, sometime later, locomotive design and construction being greatly diminished and repair being very low down the priorities. While this should have made railway workshops prime targets for enemy air raids, they were not, to my knowledge, subject to prolonged, heavy bombardment that would put them out of action. It did mean that way fewer engines were repaired and fewer built during the conflict.

Types of engines constructed during war time

The Second World War preferred locomotive. The thinking at that time was that there would come a time when the ravaged railways in Europe would instantly need motive power after we had destroyed many during air raids. Various contenders were examined, ranging from the LNER O4 Class, again, LMSR 8F and GWR 28xx classes. The engineer in charge of the procurement, Robert Arthur Riddles, opted for the LMSR design and placed an order for 240 to be delivered from May of the following year, 1940, to be built by NBL (100), Beyer, Peacock and Company (100) and by The Vulcan Foundry Limited (40). Doncaster built No. 8532. Note the steelwork for the expected electrification. (W. Potter)

The United States Amy Transportation Corps (USATC) S160 Class

An acute shortage of engines on the GWR caused by engines being sent overseas caused operational problems that threatened the service the public and government wanted. Eight hundred such locomotives were constructed in 1942/43 in the USA and shipped to South Wales and dispatched from the GWR locomotive depot at Newport, Ebbw Junction, the first forty-three locomotives being transferred to the LNER locomotive works at Doncaster for completion. This started a pattern whereby each of the four British railway companies eventually deployed a total of 400 S160s under the guise of 'running in'. but factually replacing damaged stock and increasing the capacity of the British railway system to allow for shipping of military pre-invasion equipment and troops. The eventual deployment of S160s were:

174 to the GWR
168 to the LNER
50 to the LMSR
6 to the SR

In store. This American locomotive. No. 2123 is in store at Newport, near Middlesbrough. The second batch of 400 S160s was prepared for storage by USATC personnel at the GWR's Ebbw Junction locomotive depot in the immediate run up to D-Day. After the invasion of Normandy, the locomotives deployed across Britain again began to be collected and be refurbished at Ebbw Junction in preparation for shipment to Europe. It wasn't all a bed of roses though. The high-sided tenders caused problems when coaling and the single water gauge led to several boiler explosions. (BPC)

Austerity and the War Department (WD)

An issue with the preferred engine was that it was labour and materials intensive at a time when both were in short supply. Still, this did not hinder the government from ordering the other three of the Big Four to hurry their construction; it took until three years later. During that time, the design team had come up with, some would say, a copy of the USA Class S16 in concept. It was pared down to remove all non-essentials and had its workings on the outside for ease of repairs. The small squat chimney was a design feature. Each engine saved over 6,000 man-hours compared to the previous LMSR design. As a consequence, a new Austerity engine based on the Stanier design was created and had many interchangeable parts. Locomotive production was

At Ruislip. Built from 1943 onwards, some were sent abroad (Europe and the Middle East) with BR buying some returnees and others. Class 8F, heavy freight, those engines destined for Europe were set to work here in England whilst waiting their cross-Channel trip. Passing over the water troughs on the GWR/GCR line is No. 77230. Note the Westinghouse vacuum pump on its right-hand side. It was built by the North British Locomotive Company in 1943 and was loaned to the LNER, as seen here, until hostilities ended. Several more years later and BR re-numbered it No. 90198. (BPC)

confined to making engines that were going to be essential to the war effort. Austerity was the key word, with engines made which would be stripped of all excesses and be easy to maintain. Some had the letters, 'WD' written on the cab side, those on the LNER side classified them as O7. Construction started in January 1943, and a total of 935 locomotives were built by May 1945 by the North British Locomotive Company and The Vulcan Foundry Limited works.

Southern Railway (SR)

'Coffee Pots'

This was the nickname given to these six coupled wheeled engines built in 1942, officially Q1 Class. Using the minimum amounts of raw materials, and with all superfluous features stripped away, the designer, Oliver V.S. Bulleid, produced in 1942 the most powerful steam locomotive ever to run on Britain's railways with six coupled wheels. The first twenty locomotives were constructed at Brighton Works and the remaining twenty at the company's Ashford Works. Powerful and light, the Q1s formed the backbone of the SR's heavy freight capability. The engine weighed less than 90 tons so could be used over more than 97 per cent of the SR's route mileage. All images in this section are courtesy of BPC.

The J94 Class, shunting engines. These saddle tank engines designed and built by outside engineering companies for the Ministry of Supply and became part of the stock of the LNER only after hostilities had ceased in Europe. They only scrape into this chapter as they were built (although many went straight into storage) and were only fired in peace time, most only after nationalisation, at Immingham shed. (Ted Hancock)

Feltham yard. They were later given the power classification 5F, only shared with a small number of other locomotives, such as some LNER six coupled tender engines. After construction they were given the Continental theory of numbering, painted black with yellow numbers and owner on the tender. In between duties at the yard in south London is an unidentified Q1 Class engine. (BPC)

The SR was the most financially successful of the Big Four, but this was largely based on investment in suburban and main line electrification. Having long standing senior members of the board became their Achilles heels as the railway lagged behind the others in terms of modernising its ageing fleet of steam locomotives. Following the retirement of the general manager and CME in 1937, their successors considered that the time had come to change this situation. In March 1938, CME, Oliver V.S. Bulleid, was authorised to prepare designs for twenty express passenger locomotives. A new Pacific design was settled upon instead and was intended for express passenger and semi-fast work, though it had to be equally adept at freight workings due to the nominal mixed traffic' classification Bulleid applied to the class for them to be built during wartime. Administrative measures had been put in place by the wartime government, preventing the construction of express passenger locomotives, due to shortages of materials and a need for locomotives with freight-hauling capabilities. Classifying a design as mixed traffic neatly circumvented this restriction. The SR placed an order for ten of the new locomotives to be built at Eastleigh, although the boilers had to be supplied from private industry and tenders were built at Ashford. The prototype was completed in February 1941, numbered 21C1, and named *Channel Packet* at a ceremony at Eastleigh Works on 10 March 1941. It underwent extensive trials and minor modifications before joining SR stock on 4 June 1941. A second prototype, No. 21C2, was completed in June 1941 and named *Union Castle* at Victoria station on 4 July. Both prototypes were found to be 7 tons

Merchant Navy Class. Many readers may question why I should include the Merchant Navy or 2C1 Class of engine designed by Oliver V.S. Bulleid in this section. Seeing that their distinctive air-smoothed casing aides the movement of air over the engine some would argue that this is a type of streamlining. However, they were not introduced until 1941 when the streamlined era of the other companies had been played out. The West Country and Battle of Britain classes were introduced in 1945/56, from the end of the Second World War. (BPC)

over the specified weight, and, at the insistence of the SR civil engineer, production of the remainder was halted until steps were taken to remedy this. This was achieved by using thinner steel plates for the frame and covering the boiler cladding and enlarging the existing lightening in the main frames. The remaining eight locomotives in the batch were delivered between September 1941 and July 1942.

Leader engines

The other four members of the initial order made by the SR, Nos. 36002–36005, were at varying stages of construction by the end of the development period. No. 36002 was almost complete, No. 36003 was without its outer casing, and Nos. 36004–36005 were little more than sets of frames, although most of their major components had been constructed at Eastleigh and Brighton and were stored ready for fitting. With no prospect of further money being allocated by the REC for their completion, the unfinished locomotives were put into store at various depots around the former SR network pending a decision on their future. With a calculated tractive effort of 25,350lb, the Leader Class came with the BR Class 5 power band. This was considerably lower than the contemporary Pacifics which were rated as Class 7, and this meant that the Leader Class had to be able to have an axle loading that would allow it to operate over secondary routes and on branch lines where the double-ended design would be of most benefit, something that was not likely with the weight inherent in the design. On completion, No. 36001 was immediately put into service trials using empty passenger

Leader Class project. After the Second World War, in the interregnum before nationalisation, came the controversial Leader Class design of 1946. As a concept, thirty-five units of this engine were given the go ahead with the locomotive works at Brighton starting work on the initial five. Wanting to be close to completion by the time of Nationalisation was the designer, Bulleid's, idea. Taken at Allerbrook sidings, Eastleigh is prototype locomotive No. 36001. It looks like two tank engine chassis under one boiler. The controversial idea of having driving compartments at each end was an attempt by the designer to compete with the perceived advantage that diesel engines had over steam. As mentioned in the introduction, there are examples that span different years and to catalogue them specifically is hard – this one spans different ownerships. Construction of the first five Leader Class locomotives began at the SR's Brighton Works in July 1947. BR inherited the Leader project upon nationalisation in 1948, which was far enough advanced to continue constructing the prototype, as Bulleid was still CME of the newly formed Southern Region of BR. Although work on the other four locomotives stalled, the prototype Leader Class emerged from Brighton as locomotive No. 36001 in June 1949. Despite teething troubles with the prototype, the others were initiated, only after Bulleid left for Ireland and the sister engine No. 36002 was just two days work from completion when the order was given to stop work. This was certainly a crime considering the investment already made, and it may have proved more successful than No. 36001, which was continually modified during construction. No. 36003 was considerably less finished in appearance, but still a substantial rolling chassis with boiler, when towed away to be cut up. (BPC)

LNER electric locomotive, abroad. This prototype engine No. 6701, was intended for use on the for the Woodhead line, bringing coal from Wath yard, near Barnsley, to Lancashire's homes, factories and docks. It was built at Doncaster during 1940–41 and underwent trials on the not long opened electrified (at 1,500VDC) suburban line from Manchester to Altrincham. With the Woodhead line needing major works on its tunnels, it was clear that the engine, after a spell in store at Gorton, could gain useful training experience abroad. Several countries had re-constructed their railways with overhead wires energised at 1,500VDC and so the engine was sent to Holland in September 1947. (LNER)

carriage stock in the south-east of England. The official trial records kept at Brighton Works reported varying degrees of success and failure on the runs undertaken. However, the results of the trials as reported to BR headquarters were 'conspicuous by the absence of praise' for the strengths of the Leader Class, namely the boiler, braking system and total adhesion provided by the two bogies. Several theories have been put forward regarding this state of affairs, the most plausible being that the more conservative members of the railway workforce at Brighton and the REC felt that the Leader Class was too revolutionary and were keen to maintain the status quo.

The same locomotive re-numbered 6000, worked in Holland hauling Amsterdam to Basel trains. The Woodhead line re-opened to electric trains in 1954 and this locomotive, now painted black, sporting the number 26000 and a plaque heralding the name *Tommy* returned to England.

CHAPTER 25
EFFECT OF THE WAR ON THE RAILWAYS

In some respects, the effect of another world war on the railways was similar in concept, to that of the First World War, except much greater, not only in magnitude but in geography. Below are some of the main effects that I have selected to explore in depth. As with all matter during conflicts, photographic evidence is sparce, partly due to it being illegal, unless official.

Down Street. At first, the offices of the REC were at Fielden House in Westminster. Unlike the railway companies, the GWR moved much of its management to buildings at Aldermaston, near Reading. Pictures of the accommodation, apart from the station and water troughs have been impossible to find. The company ran special trains from Paddington to Aldermaston for its staff who were planning to move their headquarters out of London. The REC remained in London to stay in close contact with the government. The basement in Fielden House was unsuitable, so the unused Down Street Tube station was converted into bomb-proof underground offices to become the headquarters of the Railway Executive Committee.

Men of the REC, April 1940. The only available space was on the platforms, but Piccadilly line trains still passed through the station. Under great secrecy, new walls were built at night when the trains had stopped running; the shape is a give-away. The doors to the new headquarters were fitted with gas locks, and short, secret, platforms were added, where REC members and senior staff could stop a train and travel in the cab to the next station. The new headquarters included offices, dormitories (with space for twelve senior officials and twenty-two members of staff), kitchens and mess rooms. The REC had a very difficult task; having been formed, they had no idea how long before war was to break out. As events turned out it was almost a year later that this happened and the minister took control from 1 September 1939 (two days before Britain declared war on Germany). The War Cabinet met here during the Blitz.

In another great respect, the management of the railways during the Second World War was very similar to the earlier one in the First World War, which precipitated the Grouping while in perspective, this second war triggered nationalisation. During both conflicts the country's railways were under the REC. This was re-formed on 24 September 1938 with a remit to run the British railways if war broke out. The railways would later be brought under government control through the REC under the direction of the Ministry of Transport.

Initially, the role of the REC was advisory and it coordinated the existing emergency plans and preparations of the railway companies and the Railway Technical Committee for such matters as civilian evacuation and ARP. (Most pictures in this chapter are unknown or courtesy of BPC except where attributed. The author endeavoured to trace all copyright holders.)

To save money on fuel and reduce the demands on the railways, the REC ordered various restrictions on passenger services, which came into effect on 11 September 1939. Passenger train services were reduced in number and speeds were restricted; various reduced fares were discontinued; reservations of seats, compartments and saloons were discontinued; restaurant car services were withdrawn; and the number of sleeping car services was reduced. REC control lasted from 1939 until the railways were nationalised in 1948.

Despite the exhortations of the government and the REC, passengers still wanted to travel, especially at holiday times. In 1943, when the summer bank holiday was at the end of July/early August, 34,000 passengers turned up at Paddington. The previous day over 40,000 tried to travel to the West Country, with all the company's trains overloaded.

One great unknown that the REC had to grapple with was the extent of air raids. Their experiences during the First World War were limited to those by Zeppelins and Gotha heavy bombers. Their range and intensity were restricted; all the minsters knew was that they were coming and going to be bigger and more destructive than before. The protection of important railway junctions was paramount, even if the efforts were limited.

Evacuation

Right from the very start, actually two days before the Second World War broke out, plans that had been developed over a year earlier were enacted. The very real threat to the civilian population resulted in programmes for moving children especially, out from city centres to safer places. In London and other major cities, adults saw long files of children led by teachers or other officials walk toward bus or train stations for their journey to different parts of the country. Each child carried around their neck a small

Evacuation. One of the most, if not the most, emotionally wrenching decisions made by the British government during the Second World War was its decision to relocate its children out of urban centres to locations where the risk of bombing attacks was low. Called Operation Pied Piper, millions of people, most of them children, were shipped to rural areas in Britain as well as overseas to Canada, South Africa, Australia, New Zealand, and the United States. Almost 3 million people were evacuated during the first four days of the operation, making it the biggest and most concentrated population movement in British history.

Arrival at 'home'. Successful as the railways' role in the mass movement of children was, by January 1940 almost 60 per cent of them had returned home. This was the 'Phoney War' period when nothing much seemed to be happening on the home front. However, when France was occupied, a second wave of evacuation began in mid-June 1940 when 100,000 children were evacuated – some for the second time. From 7 September 1940, the Blitz began and those children still in large cities were evacuated. With airbases in France available, German aircraft could penetrate deeper into England. When the Blitz began in September 1940, there were clear grounds for evacuation. Free travel and billeting allowance were offered to those who made private arrangements. They were also given to children, the elderly, the disabled, pregnant women, the ill and those who had lost their homes (some 250,000 in the first 6 weeks in London). As a result of the government and private sector efforts, London's population was reduced by almost 25 per cent. This situation lasted until the end of 1941 when cities became safer.

Above: **Moving an army.** It is hard for us to appreciate the role the railways played in moving large number of men, not to mention their equipment. Thousands of extra troop trains ferried men to the South Coast ports, and after Dunkirk, accommodated them before dispersing them to inland camps, the REC ran 620 trains carrying over 333,000 men from 7 Channel ports. To achieve this, something like 2,000 coaches were pressed into service. When the war in North Africa commenced, apart from normal trains, something like 440 troop and 680 freight trains carrying 185,000 troops, 20,000 vehicles and ¼ million tons of supplies were conveyed, again, to the ports. After the USA was dragged into the conflict, and the gradual, later, sustained build-up of men and materials for D-Day, the railways moved it all.

Opposite: **D-Day.** As with most war time photographs, there is no identity but suffice to say this is a large station. On the move are numerous troops and a few civilians as well as piles of equipment. The planning for D-Day involved the delivery, by rail, of materials and men to strategic locations. Almost overnight rural stations were swamped by miles of track and hundreds of sheds for both men and materials. The end of March 1944 was set as the date for the transportation of troops and materials to their invasion centres. Of course, during wartime there is scant pictorial record and details were scarce too. A number of false or decoy camps were built to trick the enemy. In May 1944, the LMSR ran 1,232 stores trains and the GWR 3,096. Immediately before D-Day, 4,500 trains ran with 13,000 in the following three weeks. While 40,000 troop trains had been operating in the early 1940s, by 1944 this figure had doubled and trebled as the war in Europe intensified. Imagine doing all this against a background of enemy bombing, where the lines may be blown up and the port out of action.

Ordnance on the move. The vast amounts of ordnance had to be moved, by rail, on railway wagons to ports for transfer to Europe and the Far East. Many of the country's railway factories ceased their prime job and turned to producing guns etc.

square cardboard box containing a gas mask, and on the lapel of each child's coat was pinned a name card.

Plans for such a move began during the summer of 1938, in which the country was divided into risk zones identified as 'evacuation,' 'neutral,' or 'reception' and lists of available housing were compiled. During the summer of 1939, the London County Council began requisitioning buses and trains. As the prospect of war became more likely, London's mayor, Herbert Morrison, wanted to begin the evacuation process in August, but was rebuffed by the government led by Neville Chamberlain, which was concerned that such a move would cause a general panic. Brothers and sisters held each other's hands 'like grim death and refused to be parted.' The first and largest exodus lasted four days. Other smaller evacuations occurred up until September 1944. Ultimately more than 3.5 million people were relocated. Finding homes was often traumatic for the children. As a rule, billeting officials would line the newly arrived children up against a wall or on a stage in the village hall, and invite potential hosts to take their pick. The phrase, 'I'll take that one' became a statement indelibly etched in countless children's memories. Given the large numbers and different social classes involved, individual experiences ran the gamut from excellent to terrible. There were three major evacuations in preparation for the German bombing. Operation Pied Piper started on Friday, 1 September 1939, actually two days before war broke out.

Moving the goods

Of course, it wasn't only the movement of men with which the railway became involved.

EFFECT OF THE WAR ON THE RAILWAYS

Damage to buildings

Leicester. There are a very large number of illustrations of the damage air raids did to England's towns and cities. I have selected one to give a view of the (now not so modern) desolation caused. This is Cavendish Road in Leicester.

Damage to the railway system

This is a random selection of views illustrating the damage and the conditions that the railways had to operate under. It is understood that this trail of wreckage was more by good luck rather than design. Saturation bombing, as practised by the Allies, would have paid dividends but was not pressed home by the Germans.

There were so many bombs dropped on London and the damage was so great that it would be impossible to list them all. There are a large number of pictures showing damage to buildings, stations and rollingstock, and I have selected a small number that show the effects the bombing had on lines and the ability to carry out a service.

162 • THE RAILWAY GROUPING 1923 TO THE BEECHING ERA

Above: **Newton Abbot.** This is the down platform at this important West Country station, after the air raid in 1940. There was damage to engines and to their shed. However, being such a vital crossroads on the railway system, one would have thought that a more concerted raid would have been performed. After all, it could have had the effect of curtailing traffic to Plymouth, with its dockyard, and isolating the whole of the south-west peninsula. Instead, the damage was repairable, reasonably soon. Luckily a train at the station was relatively unscathed. In a deliberate attempt to target the railways, shed and station the important junction in Devon was bombed. The damage to the station was quickly cleared away, and people were thanking their lucky stars that the bombs had not arrived a few minutes earlier. At that time, there would have been a train to Crewe at the down relief platform, on the right. As it was there 'some casualties at a South-West town', as it was reported in the local newspapers. Two of the three enemy aircraft were shot down soon after the air raid.

Opposite above: **Marshalling yard at Ferme Park, Hornsey, 1940.** This is the northern end of the station, it shows the effect one of the two bombs that fell on the station had. Notice the complete severance of the lines – up goods lines – leading to Ferme Park up yard. A small army of workmen are busily filling in the crater the blast caused. If the bombs had been a short distance nearer the yard, the ability to be repaired would have been much less than it was. Ferme Park was not restored to working order for a fortnight.

Opposite below: **Holborn Viaduct, 1941.** Looking towards Blackfriars station shows how sometimes debris looks worse than it really is. The buildings on the left took the impact of the bombs and showered the running lines with bricks. But several men and a wagon would soon have had this cleared. Had the impact been a short distance ahead, where the line crosses Ludgate Hill, the vital double junction would have put this station out of action for a considerable time.

EFFECT OF THE WAR ON THE RAILWAYS • 163

Paralysis of the port of Liverpool – almost

By 8 May, the port was at a standstill, not only due to the physical damage but a number of unexploded bombs preventing repair work and movement. Civilians were evacuated for several days. For these evacuees there were shuttle trains taking workers into the city from outlying towns and taking them home at night. Adding to all the

Opposite above: **Probably Bootle, Liverpool docks.** There was always the possibility of a 'lone wolf' attack on important visitors and so they, and the place, as secret as possible. Early the next month and for seven successive nights, the bombers targeted the docks. It is very hard to us to imagine such a situation with its apparently never-ending disruption to life. To access some of the docks, the Bootle branch went from the gridiron at Aintree, under several other lines, to the docks. Luckily, as can be seen from the picture, the line to the docks was undamaged here and so, once debris had been cleared, it could resume its function. However, further on, in Bootle docks several ships were sunk with factories and warehouses either destroyed or set on fire.

Opposite below: **Adelphi Hotel.** One feature that few people know about is how cities coordinated effects to use their resources to repair damage as quickly as possible. This is the Adelphi Hotel, in the city centre near to Central and Lime Street stations. The city was in chaos, and it is fair to say that the situation was close to collapsing, not only physically (for example, the destruction of the overhead railway over several main roads preventing transportation of debris) but also the seemingly endless pounding and inability to repair was sapping the will of the workers. It was in this hotel that the LMSR organised an information collection system but also a committee for prioritising repairs. The building itself received a hit, with casualties. During the month of May the committee met numerous times, on some days, meeting several times.

Below: **Secret visit.** The city was the second port in the country and was selected by the government to be the centre piece for the battle in the Atlantic. The Germans had also worked out that not only were their ships to destroy convoys in the Atlantic, but their bombers could have a similar effect on the docks in the city. In an attempt to boost morale, in late April 1940, Winston Churchill paid a visit to the city.

EFFECT OF THE WAR ON THE RAILWAYS • 165

Midland Adelphi Hotel, Liverpool. 4.

physical damage was the severing of all utilities, water, sewage, gas, electricity as well as telephones. If only the German information gathering service had been up to mark, it would have, at relatively little cost to their aircraft, completely put the port out of action. As it was, bombing, in the main, was minor and sporadic.

War damage around Manchester, 1940

On Christmas Eve, the line from Manchester Oxford Road to Altrincham (the joint LMSR, LNER and MSJ&AR) was severed, with some of its arches in the Castlefield district being completely destroyed. The damage could not be repaired in a short time so a plan was devised to keep the trains running. Adjacent to the joint line is the Central London Railway (CLR) line from Manchester Central, which was unscathed. In the Cornbrook area these two lines not only lie parallel to each other but also are at the same height. A plan was devised whereby a steam service shuttled from Central to Warwick Road stations. Electric trains shuttled from Altrincham to Warick Road and so by changing at the latter, access to Manchester Central could be achieved.

Heaton Norris, 1940. Two of the most miraculous escapes of the Blitz happened at Heaton Norris, a short distance south of Manchester London Road, on the main line to Crewe. Enemy bombs just missed the station buildings, leaving a large crater. The vitally important District Control Centre, housed in the station's offices was damaged but soon repaired. With the vital artery of the Stockport viaduct a short distance south of the station, damage to just a small part of it could have spelt great problems for the LMSR.

Royal Ordnance Factories (ROF)

Prior to the mid-1930s, production of ordnance was concentrated at Woolwich. However, with the potential threat from air raids, this capacity was dispersed to Waltham, Enfield as well as retaining a capacity in the Royal Arsenal in Woolwich. The siting of factories, as well as apart from centres of population, included a good transport system, chiefly railways, and access to a large workforce that could be brought in daily. The ROF needed a large area of land and although some were initiated in 1936, work only started on most in 1939. This was a reprieve for the

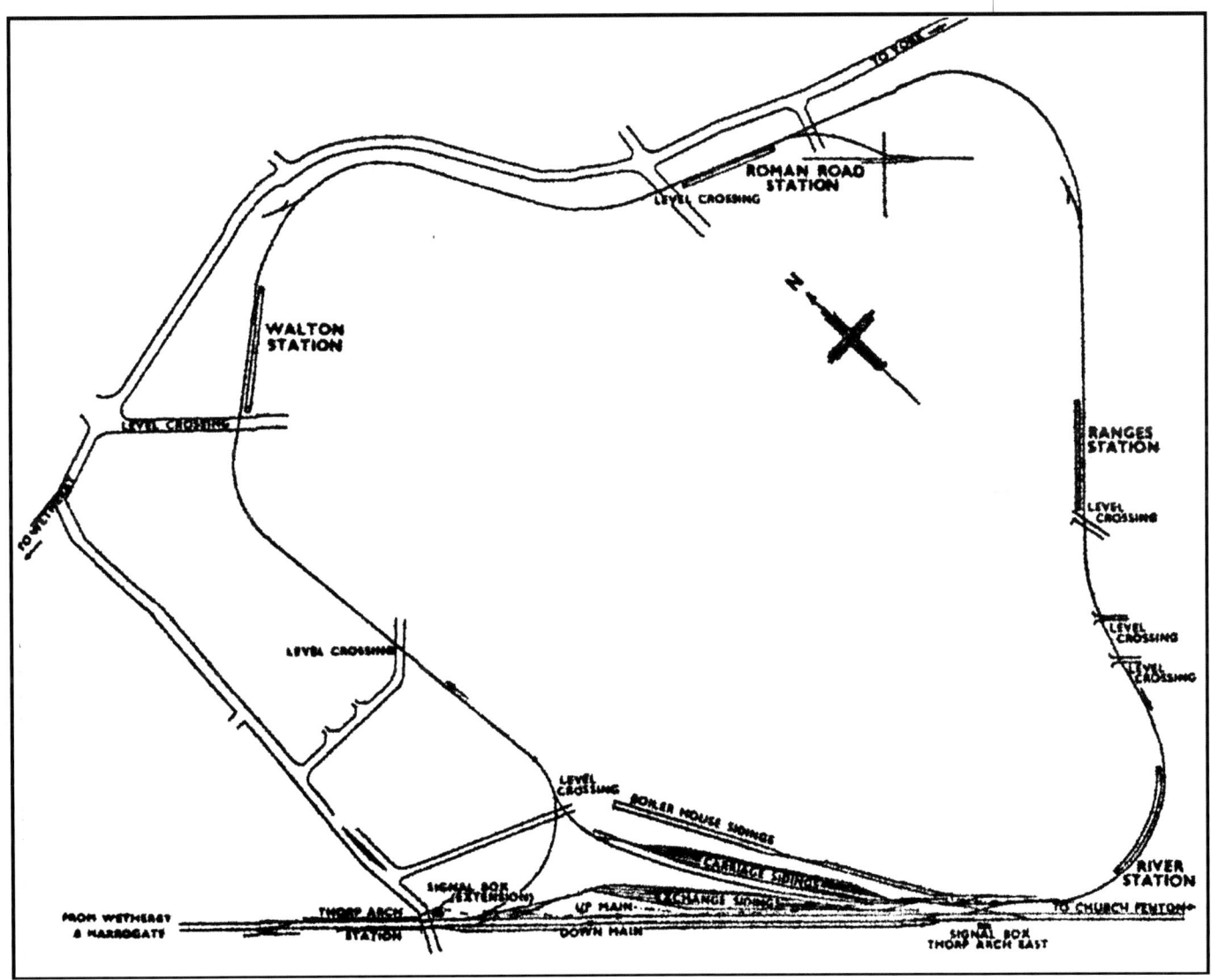

Thorp Arch filling factory (map). This is on the Harrogate to Church Fenton line in North Yorkshire, 3 miles from Wetherby. While this 450-acre site satisfied one criterion for such factories (in the countryside) it could not fulfil another (large available workforce), consequently the workforce had to be ferried in. The budget was £5.9 million and construction was expected to last eighteen months. The LNER budgeted for 18,000 men in a 24 hour period, 3 shifts of 8 hours. As well as building sidings and loops at the junction with the main line, the company also constructed a 6½ mile circular line on the site to get trains off the main lines as soon as possible. The triangular arrangement at the junction facilitated the arrival and departure of trains from both directions. Upon arrival, the trains would make a tour of the development with workers alighting at four purpose built platforms. Afterwards, the train would be stored in the carriage loops until required, at the end of the shift, to repeat the process, in reverse.

armed forces as the Munich Agreement and the 'Phoney War' both supressed the need for materials. Also, at the onset of war, many projects around the country had been stopped, calling up had not materialised on a large scale and so labourers could be diverted to the construction of these sites. At one, Cold Meece near Stoke, at its peak, 21,000 men were at work, being bussed in from nearby centres of population, chiefly, Stoke. An even bigger one at Aycliffe near Darlington, was planned to accommodate 30,000 workers but only 12,000 a day were carried. To give some perspective, the seven ROF cost was much greater than that ear-marked for the construction of aircraft.

There are three types ranging from the circular arrangement (Thorpe Arch), loops from the main line (Risley), to purpose built stations (Cold Meece).

Walton platform, 1950s. The four, single platforms consisted of earth and cinders with old wooden sleepers as facing. The other platforms were named 'Roman Road', 'Ranges' and 'River'. They had electric lighting, a nameboard and several brick shelters. The complete circular railway was brought into use on 19 April 1942 although two of the halts were operational from November 1941. From February 1941, the factory, inline with other ROF, operated a three-shift system. (Stations UK)

***Opposite below*: Women at work.** The British government introduced conscription in 1938. All men aged between 18 and 41 had to register with the government. Government officials then decided whether they should go into the army or do other war work. Most young men were recruited into the armed forces. This created a severe labour shortage and on 18 December 1941, the National Service Act was passed by Parliament. This legislation called up unmarried women aged between 20 and 30. Later this was extended to married women, although pregnant women and mothers with young children were exempt from this work. One vital need was for women to work in munitions factories. Other women were drafted to work in tank and aircraft factories, civil defence, nursing, transport and other key occupations. This involved jobs such as driving trains and operating anti-aircraft guns, that had been traditionally seen as 'men's work'. Making an urgent appeal to women to come forward for war work mainly in shell-filling factories, Ernest Bevin said he did not want them to wait for registration to take effect. He wanted a big response now, especially by those who might not have been in employment before. There was a tendency to hang back and wait for instructions. If he could get the first 100,000 women to come forward in the next fortnight it would be priceless. 'I have to tell the women that I cannot offer them a delightful life,' said Bevin. 'They will have to suffer some inconveniences. But I want them to come forward in the spirit of determination to help us through.' In districts where married women had been in the habit of doing the work, the government had decided to assist them so far as the minding of children was concerned. They had arranged for the rapid expansion through local authorities of day nurseries, and they were asking local authorities to prepare immediately a register of 'minders'. The married woman would pay only what she paid in pre-war days – about sixpence a day – and the government would pay an additional sixpence a day for looking after the children. All these activities put a strain on the railways that they rose to the occasion, but it was unsustainable. The government's promise to reimburse the railways to a pre-war level was broken from 1941.

Risky business. Working at ROF carried risks and although this picture is probably from an earlier conflict, the risks were greater during the Second World War. There were two explosions at Kirkby ROF, one in February 1944 and one on 15 September 1944. Two people were killed in the first accident, and fourteen killed and eleven injured in the second. It took three months of work to clear 4,000 bombs, which were buried in the rubble after the second accident resulting in a total of thirty-seven awards for bravery and distinguished conduct.

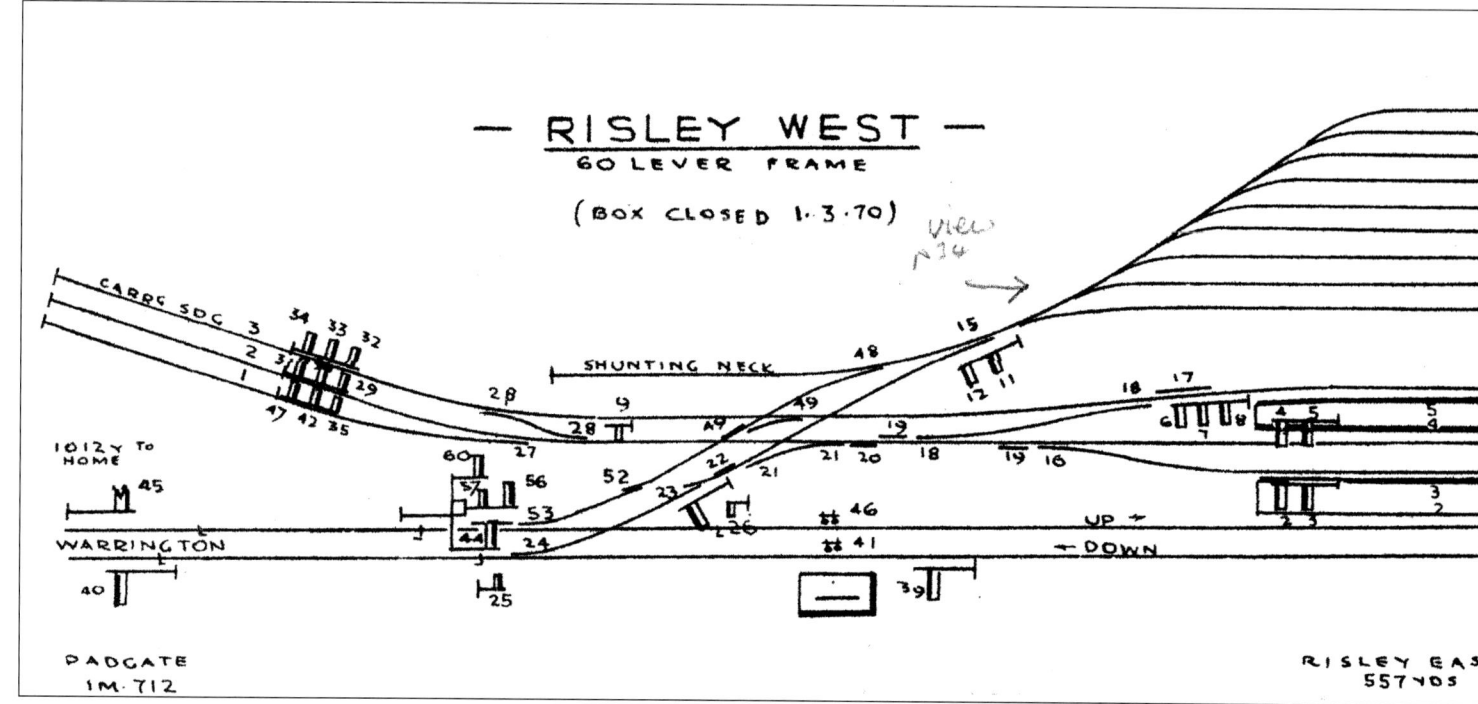

Risley. To give some ides of the scale of the undertaking, here is the track layout at the ROF at Risley, near Warrington. Notice how it can be accessed from both up and down directions. At the down end of the layout there is provision for storage of coaches while people are working. At the up end are engine release facilities to free engines having brought carriages. This was 'Filling factory No. 6'. With the advent of the war, 927 acres of largely heath and moss land which was part of Risley village that was compulsorily purchased and within it was built a large ROF. The location was chosen because the low lying mist and cloud helped hide the factory from the air. A part of the site was drained, and construction began in August 1939. It took eighteen months to complete, but bombs were produced from September 1940.

Risley was a filling factory. It received the explosives in bulk, usually by rail, from other ROFs where they were manufactured. Here the finished munitions were made by filling the casings. It was one of sixteen filling factories around the country, others in the north west included Chorley (No. 1) and Kirkby (No. 7). A feature common to all of the filling factories was an area of storage bunkers where the finished munitions were stored awaiting dispatch. The areas within the filling factories were all numbered in the same way. Risley had twenty such bunkers and Area 9, storage bunker area, is roughly in the area of the main field in Birchwood Forest Park today. When the new town area of Birchwood was created, most of the bunkers were demolished, but four of them were left in place and can still be seen today.

A number of bunkers were also built to house the munitions, to protect them from potential bombing, and also to segregate the site and reduce the consequences of any accidental explosions during manufacture or storage. Although these bunkers are on the surface, they are covered with soil and turf and so give the impression of being underground. It had a dedicated rail link to the Manchester-Wigan branch, which was used both for bringing in workers and moving materials. Also there was a halt on the Liverpool-Manchester line. There was a constant threat that not only would the site be the target for enemy bombers, if they knew of its existence, but from accidents on site causing explosions.

EFFECT OF THE WAR ON THE RAILWAYS • 171

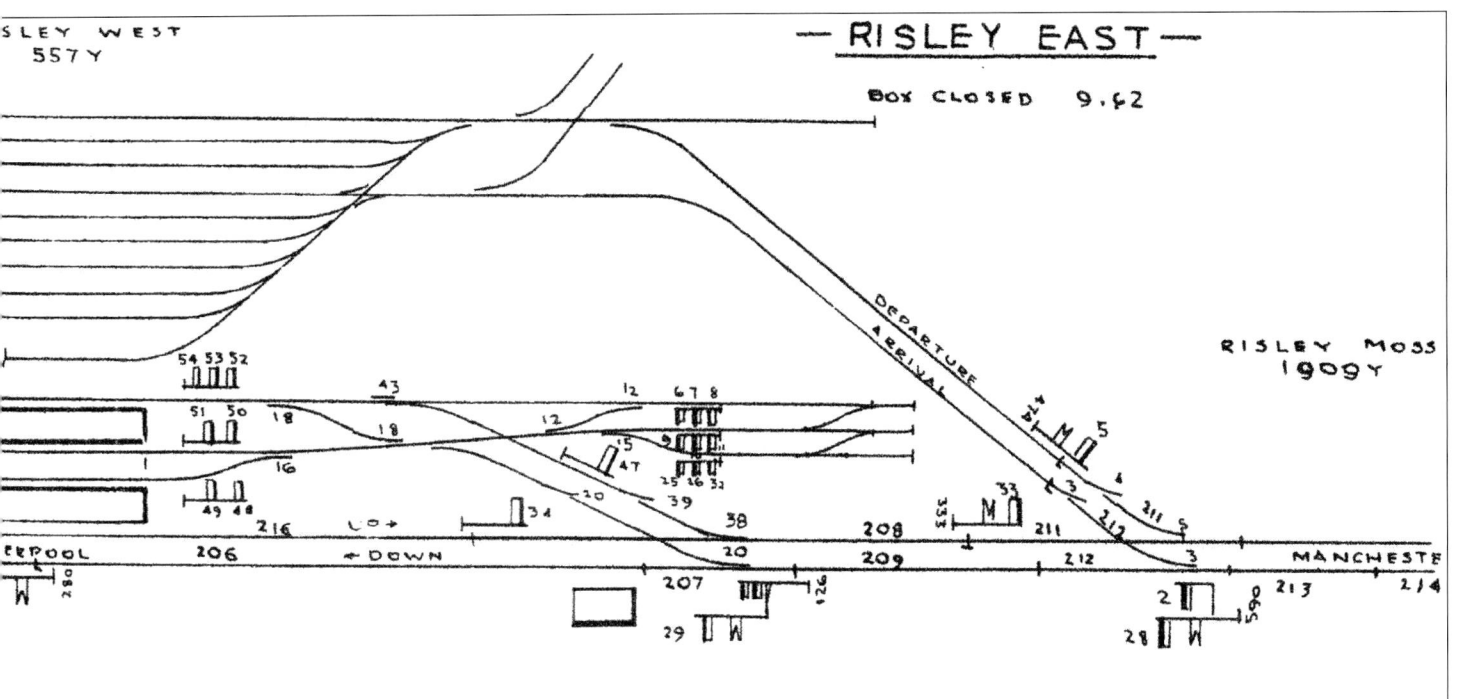

Sidings at Sankey Junction. West of the junction between the Cheshire Lines Railway's lines of the 'direct' (Manchester to Liverpool) and the 'straight line' (serving Warrington Central) and the line crosses over both the Sankey Brook Navigation Canal and Sankey brook. West of these bridges was a site chosen by the Air Ministry when war broke out for the site of a new aircraft repair depot. The main line is on the left, facing Liverpool. Interesting are the gates showing the end of the joint line and the ownership of the Air Ministry. Beyond are eight loops with wagons with their connections to the main line controlled by the signal post with three doll arms. These allowed trains from the depot to use a head-shunt (top signal pulled 'off'), head towards Manchester or to back onto the down main line. If performing the latter operation, the train would have to block both lines before setting off for Liverpool. (BPC)

New lines during the Second World War

Oxford

Above: **Heading north.** Coming towards our position is a train of empty wagons, partially obscured by its smoke; LMSR engine No. 4227. Straddling the branch of the River Thames is a goods train. It is held at the up signals by the junction, the GWR's goods depot in the town is south of the station. Operations at the junction started to cause congestion and so a pair of loops, a short distance north were laid in 1941. Hidden in the smoke is a new ARP designed brick signal box, named North Junction.

Opposite above: **South of the city.** To the south of the city in the low lying land prone to flooding and prior to the branch east to Princes Risborough a set of marshalling sidings were laid down at Hinksey, in 1942, taking over the site of the long abandoned Hinksey Halt. Looking south from the interestingly named, Devils Backbone footbridge captures an unknown passenger train passing the sidings, on the right. Controlling events was a specially built GWR air raid precaution signal box, Hinksey, with 14inch walls and a flat concrete roof. It had wood rather than the customary metal window frames.

EFFECT OF THE WAR ON THE RAILWAYS • 173

Other North-South links

Apart from the main lines, there were other minor lines that were pressed into service in the run-up to D-Day, giving access to Southampton and the Channel ports.

Bordesley. This is where the ex-MR line across Birmingham passes over the GWR main line to the city. A single line connection allowed transfer of goods between the two systems. In 1941 it was decided to double the link so improving flow of goods. Light engine, No. 7929 *Wyke Hall*, a product of a 1944 locomotive building programme by the GWR, is passing from its own metals along the chord.

South from Didcot

A branch line departed from the east of Didcot station and turned south towards Newbury. The line was a crucial transport link as southern England saw huge movements of troops and military supplies, with intensive use in 1944. In preparation, extensive capacity enhancement works were undertaken, and the line was temporarily closed in the daytime between 4 August 1942 and 8 March

Worthy Down platform. This was opened to the public in October 1920 having been built by the GWR on 1 April 1918. Its purpose was to serve an adjacent army camp and it had two passing loops, following the 1943 works, including opening this thirty lever brick signal box. At its peak the line was carrying 120 train movements a day. The loops are serving just that purpose as viewed from an adjacent road bridge, with a GWR train on the right and a northbound ten-coach passenger train on the other line at the island platform. The shorter loop was used to unload wagons for the camp. Later, the station became a junction for a spur to connect with the SR's main line through to Winchester. At the junction, an additional line was built on the opposite side of the station to provide an island platform serving both northbound and southbound trains on separate lines. The flat terrain meant that the area was eyed by the War Office as a suitable disembarkation area for troops after Dunkirk and a short lived single platform halt existed at Barton Stacey near here from February to December 1940 for that purpose. Apart from serving the camp, it is unclear if the public trains stopped here. The Sutton Scotney services on the A34 is now in the area.

1943; during this period this section was doubled, as was the first 2 miles south of Newbury. Down on the right is the brick built signal box containing twenty-three levers. This 1943 ARP model has a concrete flat roof and thick concrete beams over the windows; all designed to withstand enemy bombs although it did not stop water penetration. The steps were inside the structure. A footbridge was built at the same time. Trains from Southampton's docks, heading north, destined for Didcot and the Midlands, had to cross over the busy SR lines, south of Winchester, at Shawford Junction. A chord was built in 1943 from just after the Didcot line had been passed over by the SR line near Winchester Junction, to connect with the lower line near Worthy Down platform.

At the end of the war

Reverse evacuation. Having ferried numerous children (some more than once) adults, soldiers to France, and back, and again as well as vast quantities of ordnance, one may have thought the railways deserved a rest. Well, there were all the displaced people in this country who needed to go home. This recent commemorative stamp pays tribute to the system that re-united families.

Woman, the war, and work

'Women's work'. Due to the number of deaths, mostly to men, during the First World War, there was a serious shortage of men, not only from the country's perspective of families, but also from the idea of a workforce. Of course, factories and other employers started to employ women in even greater numbers. Contrary to general belief, the railways were not an all-male preserve. In the rural areas many women ran the railways, contributing to the around 26,000 women at the start of the Second World War in 1939, amid attitudes of the time that women should not work outside the home if their husbands were employed, and that working women were taking jobs away from men who needed them more. In towns and cities women did work in engineering works as long as they stuck to 'feminine' jobs. As the war progressed, the number of working women increased as there was simply a scarcity of men, and by D-Day over 110,000 women were employed.

The unions agreed to this on the proviso that women worked on starter grades, and they were to relinquish their roles when the men came home. With many jobs being split into several parts, it gave rise to the phrase, 'three women to do one man's job'. This breaking the concept of women at work was accepted for the duration, however, the genie was out of the bottle and would never be bottled up again.

Driving. Of course, it was not only unskilled men that went to fight, but many skilled men too. To replace them, women became trained in technical jobs. It wasn't only the men who found employment on new vehicles, such as this Scammel three-wheeler motor unit. With its ability to turn in tight corners it really was able to take over from the horse and cart. Prior to the war, the concept of women drivers was extremely rare, most men could not drive either. This mirrors in some way, the situation at the end of the First World War regarding men with a new skill, driving, entering the labour market.

Track maintenance. Many women were employed in manual jobs that men formerly did. At Reading women are maintaining the track in 1943.

Bevan boys

Mining. These were sometimes called 'the forgotten conscripts'. With as many as possible able men conscripted to the armed forces, the mining industry suffered a shortage of miners. Under emergency legislation, miners were banned from being recruited into the armed forces. Some 30,000 ex-miners were sent back to work in the pits. Absenteeism became a problem and neither the special efforts of Churchill, the prime minister, nor a special visit by the King and Queen to the Doncaster coalfield had much effect; by 1945 the figure had risen to one in six men not at work. It needs to be remembered that mining at that time was dependent on men hewing out the coal, loading it into tubs, which were pushed, or pulled by ponies, and lifted to the surface. It was hot, hard and dangerous work. Against this background is the statistic that some of the pits in the South Yorkshire coalfield each produced around 1 million tons of coal each year. In 1943, Britain faced a crisis in coal production as there was only three weeks of coal stock available. This put the country's ability to win the war in jeopardy. Winston Churchill charged Ernest Bevin, Minister of Labour and National Service to increase coal production. Bevin decided that from all 18 to 24 year old men conscripts drafted to serve in the armed forces one in ten were to be directed – on pain of imprisonment and irrespective of background or ability – to work underground in British coal mines. In 1943 it was announced that a ballot scheme upon registering for National Service, would be selected according to the last digit of his registration number to serve in the pits. Approximately 48,000 Bevin Boys (as they came to be known) undertook unskilled manual jobs to release more experienced miners to move on to coal production at the coal face. As they did not go to fight, an unfortunate stigma was attached to them, but they were not 'conchies' nor draft dodgers or deserters. Some, due to local hostility were arrested as foreign agents. Many men so drafted were reluctant and ill-disciplined, refusing to comply and 143 were imprisoned. Unlike those who had served in the military, Bevin Boys were not awarded medals for their contribution to the war effort and official recognition by the British government was only conferred in 1995.

Skilling women. One vital need was for women to work in munitions factories. Other women were conscripted to work in tank and aircraft factories, civil defence, nursing, transport and other key occupations. This involved jobs such as driving trains and operating anti-aircraft guns, that had been traditionally seen as 'men's work'.

A workforce was needed to make the armaments and the guns that the front line troops needed. There were not the men to make the aircraft, so women were drafted in to perform these tasks. Some women were conscripted into various roles away from their homes. One young lady was drafted from a village in Cornwall to work on aircraft production in Swindon. This meant training women to do highly skilled tasks.

Gratifying as men found it to be served by a woman at a tea stand on a station, women were well and truly in the market for employment-once the war was won. In the 1920s, more than 8 million women, or one in five, were earning salaries, typically as clerks, waitresses, teachers and telephone operators.

CHAPTER 26
THE LEGACY OF THE GROUPING

Railways after the Second World War and the origins of British Railways

A decade after the Grouping and the Big Four railway companies were beginning to iron out decades of rivalry and to work as large, united sets of companies. They were innovative and forward looking. The reign of George VI brought about possibly the biggest upheavals the railways had experienced. What caused this?

World War, Again

The Big Four companies would never really recover from the consequences of the First World War. While many of the designs of the 1920s and 1930s had demonstrated just how capable they were of maintaining maximum performance with a minimum of outlay, the whole railway system was on its knees. The companies' income during the First World War had been capped and once the conflict was over, they simply did not have the resources to cope with the enormous backlog of repairs and reconstruction which had built up over the previous six years.

One person unlikely to get a positive mention around this time was Sir Eric Geddes. However, Geddes, an admiral and cabinet minister, admired by the prime minister and others at that time, led to the belief that his views were correct for the industry. There are some who would maintain that the real grouping took place as nationalisation. All of the regions produced a working surplus well into the mid-1950s. At the Grouping the ruthless plans regarding duplicate routes and stations was not put into action, it not being enacted some thirty years or more later. Why was this? Some would believe that the Grouping was a pet project of Geddes. The plan was unnecessary, its conception flawed, its planning and its execution muddled; all it had was a simplicity to its result. If nationalisation had been implemented then with a sound economic base, the need for profitability would not have been necessary. Another possible plan was for the railway companies to carry on as they were before the conflict although afterwards and during the economic conditions during the recession there would have been some takeovers and the removal of duplicated lines. Geddes's died in 1926.

There were social upheavals too. Never before had so many women worked in so many jobs formerly done by men. A 'stock check' of the four companies on the brink of nationalisation would reveal that the largest company, the LMSR, employed more people than the peace time British Army and owning twenty-eight hotels it was the biggest operator of railway hotels in the world. Next was the LNER's who's staple traffic was freight and although it was renowned for its streamlined expresses it was the least revenue earner of the cohort at £1,749 per route mile. The most modern of the four, although running mostly passenger services, the SR generated the most revenue at almost double that of the worst performer. With revenue only 10 per cent greater than the worst performing company, the GWR had tentacles from London, southern England and most of Wales and its staff were fiercely loyal to the brand.

The shape of things to come

By 1947, with a Labour government in power after its landslide election victory of 1945, proposals for nationalising the railways became a reality, and on 1 January 1948 the era of the Big Four was over although its legacy would endure until BR's Modernisation Plan of 1955 started to come into fruition.

No. 10000, the early years. The LMSR engine No. 10000 was officially presented to the press at Derby Works on 8 of December 1947, having emerged from the works on 5 December for the first time. The official handing-over ceremony of No. 10000 occurred at Euston on 18 December 1947, at which Sir George Nelson, the chairman and managing director of The English Electric Company Limited, and Sir Robert Burrows, the chairman of the LMSR, spoke of 'the importance of the experiment'. The timing of the hand-over (just prior to nationalisation) was chosen with some deliberation as the LMSR was keen to see that their new diesel locomotive – being entirely LMSR in origin – should bear the company's insignia in traffic. The former CME of the LMSR, Sir William Stanier, was also at the handing-over ceremony, to attend the unveiling of his nameplates on brand new, penultimate Pacific No. 6256. How was this new nationalised railway greeted? At Euston station an un-named Patriot Class engine No. 5508 left with a train for Crewe, all very low key. In Paddington station, at five minutes into the new era, No. 5032 *Usk Castle* departed with a train for Birkenhead accompanied by a climax of exploding detonators on the line; a much more spectacular event. (BPC)

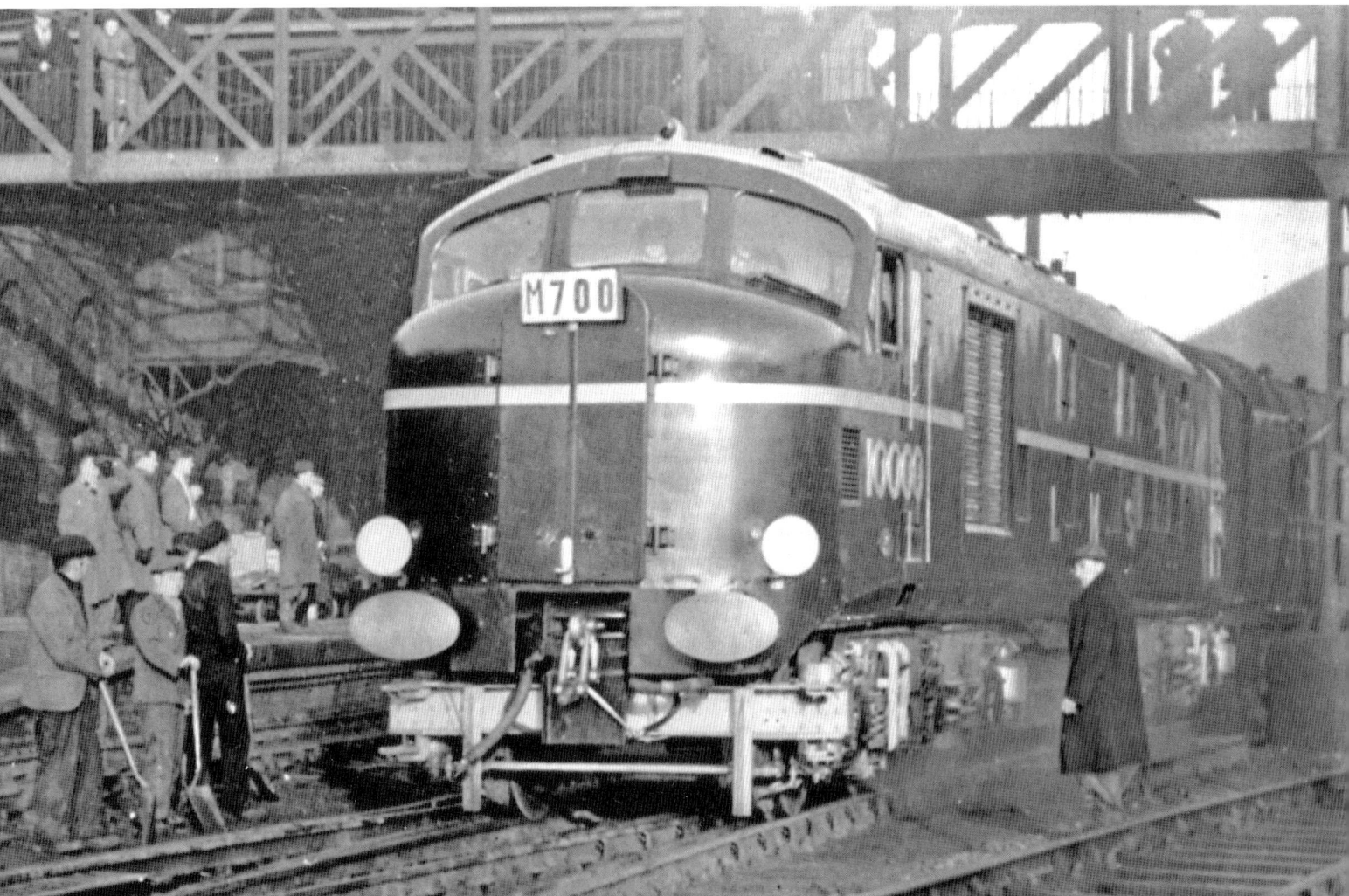

Anti-nationalisation. Two factors were brought to bear on the fate of the railways after the Second World War was over. Britain found that the railways were indispensable by necessity; the country simply could not have succeeded without a government controlled system. On the other hand was a philosophical idea that such an important business should be run for the benefit of the people and not to the vagaries of the stock market. Followers wanted the railways to be indispensable by choice, 'a people's railway'. With the railways short of capital, it would be impossible for them to re-build the system without borrowing on a scale that could not be repaid. In a similar situation after the First World War, the only lender of such capital was the government; the price would be public ownership. The chairmen of the Big Four devised a campaign against nationalisation arguing that the business case had not been made and that it was only a political act, one which in later years may have a profound effect. With many of the most influential posts held by elder statemen it was the lower ranks, made of younger men to argue the case for public control. Opposing this was the emerging road haulage lobby. A 'landlord and tenant' scheme was put forward by the two largest companies, the LMSR and the LNER which was gaining some success. However, the chairman of the largest, the LMSR, changed his mind and that idea came to nothing. Consequently, the British Transport Commission (BTC) started life in an attic of the LT offices at 55 Broadway, London. (BPC)

THE STATE
AND
THE RAILWAYS

AN ALTERNATIVE TO NATIONALISATION

Memorandum by the Board of the London and North Eastern Railway Company

October, 1946

Nationalisation

Railways after the Second World War

It is all very well suggesting a unison between different companies but an altogether different matter for this to happen as there were so many different fractions. 'One of the key issues was that while there was the opportunity in 1923, after the First World War to re-draw the railway map and 'trade' lines to avoid geographical anomalies, such as the GWR and SR in the south-west, as well as come to agreement over duplicated lines was missed, here was another chance to put matters sensibly.

On a practical level, the system was in poor physical shape. It could not all be repaired at once so which areas should be done first? Steel rationing did not cease until the mid-1950s, and railways had to take their place in the nationalised life, steel, coal, hospitals, schools etc.

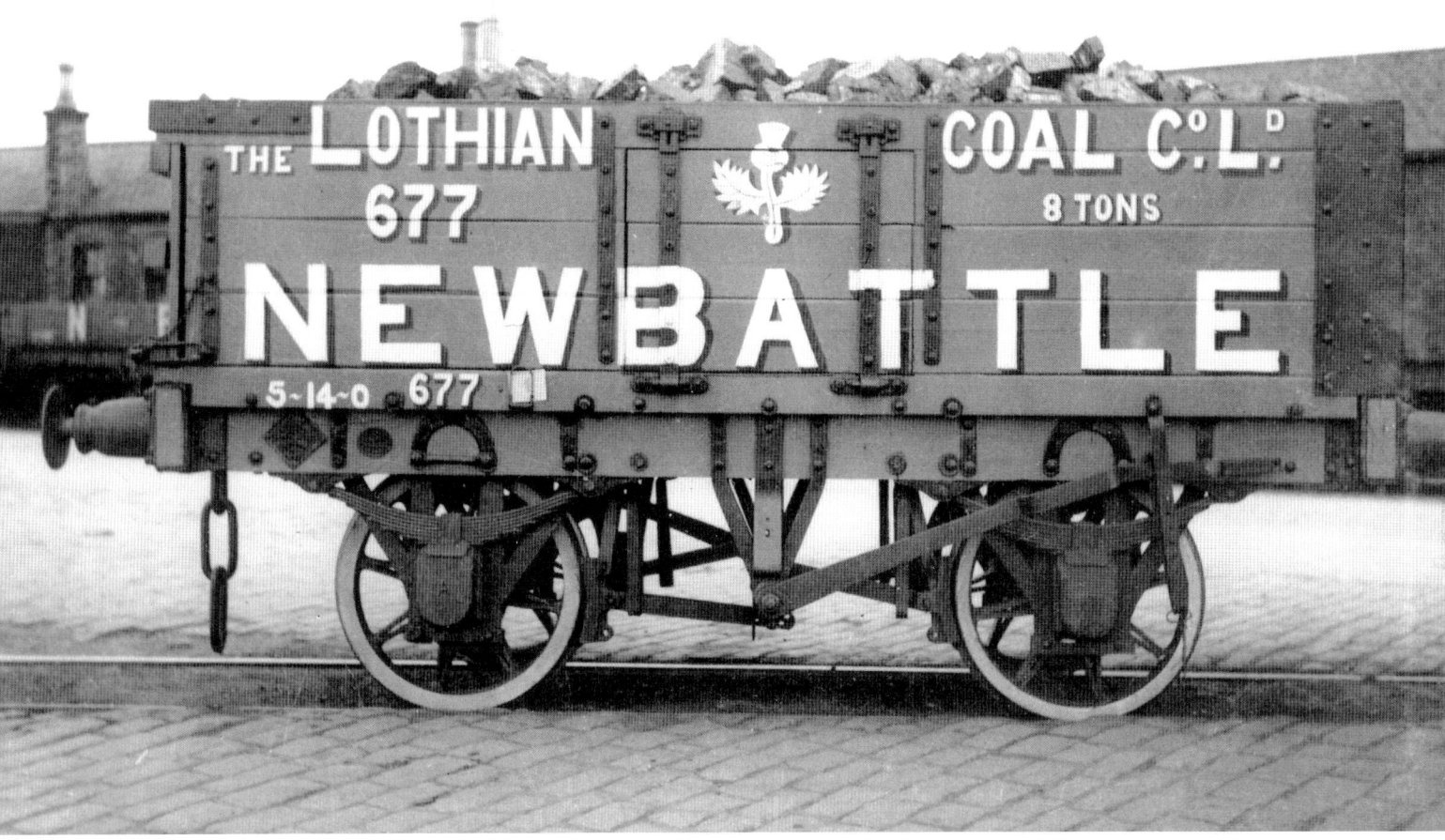

Private owners wagons. One issue that illustrates the lack of hard nosed business attitude that the BTC had was regarding wagons. In 1948 there were around ½ million of them, mostly owned by colliery owners. It was their job to sell coal and BTC's role was to transport the coal. So, the responsibility to move the coal rested with a body that had no wagons. So the BTC bought the wagons (£159 for a 'new' [re-built within last five years] wagon.) However, the BTC predicted that within a few years they could fulfil their role with a lot fewer (85,000) wagons than they had recently acquired. By the mid-1950s, around half of the bought wagons were obsolete – the taxpayer had been taken for a ride so eroding the principle of nationalisation with financial concerns. (R.K. Blencowe)

Similarly, rolling stock and coaches needed replacement and modernisation. The locomotive stud consisted of over 100 different designs, inherited from the Big Four. Engines had been damaged and poorly maintained during the Second World War so replacements were needed. There was not an 'off the shelf' engine readily available, so which ones should they build to replace those damaged?

However, on the Continent, pre-war programmes had centred on electrification while across the pond, dieselisation was rapidly replacing steam. Should the board stick with steam or go for these other modes of power.

In the background were petrol driven engines. Even though petrol was rationed until 1953, they were making rapid inroads both in private cars (2 million in 1939, 2.75 million in 1953, 7 million in 1963) and commercial lorries. Both types of vehicles

184 • THE RAILWAY GROUPING 1923 TO THE BEECHING ERA

***Above*: Re-using old technology on the Lickey Incline, 1949.** Incidentally, the steep gradient from Wath yard to the Woodhead tunnel led the LNER in 1926 to produce a new engine, actually two motor units under one massive boiler. When the route was electrified far fewer electric engines and crews were needed. What to do with this purpose built banking engine? Still with some life in it, it was sent to the ex-LMSR system to help push trains up the notorious Lickey Incline towards Birmingham in May 1949. Here the train has crested the incline at Blackwell and the banker, which had buffered up behind the train, has shut off steam and is slowing down. Soon it will stop and reverse onto the other line, descend the incline to wait at Bromsgrove for its next assignment. After varying degrees of success, after servicing in Yorkshire, it was converted to oil burning, and tried on the Lancashire side of the Woodhead line to push trains, and so reduce the time of their line occupation, towards the tunnel. An oil crisis later that decade put paid to not only this experiment but to others where locomotives had been converted to oil burning, later to be re-converted in April 1954. Although BR were willing to look at different ways of doing things, it also illustrated one of the chief reasons for the downfall of the Woodhead route; envisaged in the late 1930s but not fully operational for another twenty years. A booklet published just after nationalisation by the Liberal Party advocated electrification of the ex-GCR main line down to Marylebone. Some would say that this was the real purpose of the electric locomotives of Class EM2 as they were really superfluous for passenger services on the short Manchester to Sheffield line. (Millbrook House)

***Opposite above*: Locomotive remnant.** When the railways emerged from the Second World War they inherited schemes that had their origin not for the speedy transit of goods and people necessitated by the war, but schemes that were started in the late 1930s. The most celebrated one is the electrification of the coal route from Wath yard, in Yorkshire, through the Pennines to the homes, factories and docks in Lancashire. With little done prior to 1939, apart from the erection of steel supports for the later electrified wires, the government was committed to complete the scheme. As most readers will be aware, this involved boring a new tunnel through the Pennines and so the scheme only really became operational in 1954. Apart from new engines to haul the coal trains, which saved precious coal, the BTC decided that they needed a new engine, ostensibly to haul passenger trains. With a 60mph limit imposed on the route and the existing fleet capable of coping with the passenger/freight demands of the day, there seemed little point in using time, expertise, materials and money on producing a new design. The booklet advocated complete electrification of the former GCR main line down to Marylebone. That would justify larger than No. 26000 series locomotives, like the one illustrated. So, maybe, the design work would not have been wasted. As it was, only a small group of seven such engines were produced, here No. 27000, later named *Electra* is in store at Wath yard awaiting work in 1954. (RAS)

were coming over the horizon and were having, and would have a bigger, impact on railways' business than could not be ignored.

A golden opportunity was created for the railways between 1947 and the ending of petrol rationing. With a great advantage over motor vehicles then with foresight, the nettle could have been grasped so creating a situation that could last for a long time. All that stood in the way was amalgamation. Management of this new company was an issue. Some experts wanted there to be no regional administration, calling it a, 'not a practicable option', others wanted a return to the Big Four while the mood music was to have six regions. A new area, Scottish, was to be created from parts of the old LNER and the LMSR, and the ex-LNER was to be split into a North Eastern and Eastern zones. There was speculation as to the viability of the new North Eastern Region – was it too small to survive? The issue of who ruled in Cornwall, SR or GWR, still had not been broached. Trying to get four large companies to work together was difficult enough in 1923 but now there were to be six and as some companies experienced earlier, would preoccupy the minds of managers rather than looking to the future. Taking their eyes off the ball meant that the Modernisation Plan for the railways did not appear until 1955. By this time, most of the railways of Continental Europe had electrified their important lines and were planning to replace all their steam locomotives. After many years of wrangling, BTC was locked into a programme whereby steam would not be replaced completely until the later 1960s.

One matter that would become a stick with which to beat the railways was finances. While the setting up mantra was 'economical' this was later, by more conservative politicians, to mean 'profitable'. The originators of the Transport Act 1947 were more concerned with the country having a transport service sensing that an inefficient one was to the country's detriment. Future politicians translated this in ton per mile and footfall per train; being publicly owned it was the people's railway that should be run properly, not an accountant's haven. Of course, such a large undertaking, as a country entire transport system, needed managers of vision and nerve with politicians to match-both working in the public interest.

British Road Services (BRS)

As well as the Ian Allan *ABC of Locomotives* there was one that contained a list of British Road Services depots, fleet codes that youngsters spotted in the early 1950s, much the same way that they had spotted railway engines.

Freight on the roads. As a result of the Transport Act 1947, Britain's road haulage industry was nationalised in 1948 as BRS. The nationalised transport operator became one of the biggest road transport companies in the UK during the 1950s. As with railways, political interference greatly affected the company with partial de-nationalisation, BRS, along with its parcels and other divisions, continued to be a major part of the transport scene up to the 1980s, when it was split up. In parallels with the railways, collecting the lorry numbers became a popular pastime during the early years. Later, by the 1960s, it was made up of four main operating areas: British Road Services Limited, BRS (Parcels) Limited, Pickfords, and Containerway and Roadferry Limited. The road haulage industry was in its infancy and in the hands of numerous one-man bands, with the men loading up and going wherever the load demanded. After dropping it off, there then became a desperate search for a return load, often driving across the country to a port or BRS depot, not knowing when the driver would be home. The system was very different then with no central distribution hubs etc. There were no maximum driving hours in those days, with drivers often sleeping in the cab to save money on bed and breakfast. Drivers would arrive home, often in the wee small hours, stay a couple or at the most three days, and then be off again for another extended period of time. (BPC)

Poster. An inventory taken at the cessation of hostilities in 1945 would have shown that the railway industry was badly in need of attention. Much of the permanent way needed repair as did the rolling stock, as much as one third. To compound the problem there was a severe shortage of materials – steel was not 'off rations' until 1956 – and there was a shortage of manpower. Although many women filled roles vacated by men, the more skilled jobs could not be filled easily as it would take time, and social attitudes to change, before women could fill the labour gaps left by the casualties of the war. The immediate post-war election returned a government with a mandate for public ownership and the railways were competing with other industries for men, materials and money. This poster being pasted up heralded the new order: 'Founded: 1 January 1948'. Actually, the Transport Act 1947 that produced this one large company arrived on 6 August 1947 and so there was a gap between that date and the vesting day. During that time the order was 'carry on as normal' in true British fashion. There were some restrictions on land sales and a ban on certain contracts being signed. Following the Transport Act, to manage the country's transport, a new business, BTC, was created. It was responsible for roads, canals and air traffic as well as railways. (BPC)

The old order changeth: the first poster announcing transfer of the railways to the British Transport Commission

Clement Atlee. Attlee took Labour into the wartime coalition government in 1940 serving under Winston Churchill, eventually, as deputy prime minister from 1942. When the war cabinet headed by Churchill was dissolved and elections were held, the Labour Party led by Attlee won a landslide victory in the 1945 general election on a post-war platform of recovery. Following the election, Attlee led the construction of the first Labour minority government. His government's approach was to maintain full employment while aiming to maintain a greatly enlarged system of social services provided by the state. To this end, it undertook the nationalisation of public utilities and major industries, and implemented wide-ranging social reforms. He brought forward ideas of how to merge the Big Four into a unified BR in 1946. (BPC)

CHAPTER 27
THE EVENTFUL 1950s

Festival of Britain, 1951

***Opposite above*: Festival.** After the euphoria of victory, not only in the Second World War but by electing a 'people's government', everyone expected the country to be on its former footing sooner. The Labour government was losing support and so to give the people a feeling of a successful recovery from the war's devastation, as well as promoting British science, technology, industrial design, architecture and the arts, a festival was mooted. Having had the plan for some years, Labour cabinet member Herbert Morrison, the prime mover, in 1947, started with the original plan to celebrate the centennial of the Great Exhibition of 1851. However, it was not to be another world fair, for international themes were absent, as was the British Commonwealth. Instead, the 1951 festival focused entirely on Britain and its achievements. It was funded chiefly by the government, with a budget of £12 million. Just six years after the end of world war, Britain's towns and cities still showed the scars of war that remained a constant reminder of the turmoil of the previous years. With the aim of promoting the feeling of recovery, the Festival of Britain was opened by the king and queen on 4 May 1951, celebrating British industry, arts and science and inspiring the thought of a better Britain. The main site of the festival was constructed on a 27 acre area on the South Bank, London, which had been left untouched in the six years since being bombed in the war; it proved to be a perfect time to showcase the principles of urban design that would feature in the post-war rebuilding of London and other towns and cities. The main site featured the largest dome in the world at the time, standing 93ft tall with a diameter of 365ft. Other buildings at the festival site on South Bank include the Royal Festival Hall, a 2,900 seat concert hall that hosted opening concerts conducted by Sir Malcolm Sargent and Sir Adrian Boult; a new wing of the Science Museum holding the Exhibition of Science; and, located nearby, The Exhibition of Live Architecture at Poplar. Upriver, only a few minutes via boat from the main Festival site, was Battersea Park. This was home to the funfair part of the festival. This included pleasure gardens, rides and open-air amusements.

Although the main site of the festival was in London, the festival was a nationwide affair with exhibitions in many towns and cities throughout Britain. This included such exhibitions as the Industrial Power Exhibition in Glasgow and the Ulster Farm and Factory Exhibition in Belfast, not to forget the Land Travelling Exhibition and the Festival Ship Campania that travelled from town to town and city to city around Britain. Celebrations, parades and street parties took place all around the country.

As with most large government-sponsored and funded projects (the Millennium Dome and the London Olympics in 2012 spring to mind), the festival met with much controversy, from the concept to completion. Even before the festival opened, it was condemned as a waste of money. Many people believed it would have been better spent on housing after the destruction of many houses during the Second World War. Once opened, the critics turned to the artistic taste; the Riverside restaurant was seen as too futuristic, the Royal Festival Hall seen as too innovative and even certain furnishings in the café met criticism for being too gaudy. It was also criticised for being too expensive, with entrance to the Dome of Discovery at 5 shillings. Even with the above complaints the main festival site on the South Bank managed to attract more than 8 million paying visitors. (BPC)

***Opposite below*: New engine.** One railway exhibit that can be seen attracting a lot of attention was one for the future. This electric engine, No. 26020, completed out of sequence so that it could be exhibited in London, is intended to haul trains, especially those laden with coal, from Wath marshalling yard in Yorkshire into Lancashire, for consumption or export. (BPC)

THE EVENTFUL 1950s • 189

SOUTH BANK EXHIBITION
FESTIVAL OF BRITAIN, 1951

Above: **New Woodhead tunnel.** The engine, above, also hauled the first train through the Woodhead tunnels after a special opening ceremony. Incidentally, it is the engine chosen to represent the class in the national collection at York; somehow the named locomotive, which spent its early years in Holland earning it the name, *Tommy*, seems to have been overlooked. The new Woodhead tunnel was one of three parallel Trans-Pennine 3-mile long tunnels linking Yorkshire with Derbyshire. The original single tunnel, later paired, had become an operational liability as time went on. The continuous pounding of the brick lining led to many bricks becoming dislodged and there was a continual programme of weekend single-line activity to repair the damage. When it was proposed to electrify the line between Wath yard through to similar yards to the west it was discovered that the tunnels could not accommodate the necessary equipment, hence a new, double-track tunnel was built. Unlike the older ones which had a curve in them, this new one was straight. (BPC)

Opposite above: **Named train.** The name *Royal Wessex* was inaugurated by the Southern Region of BR to mark that year's Festival of Britain. Before the Second World War, a named train, *Bournemouth Limited,* a successor to the SR provided a two-hour express to the coastal resort. Reinstated on 3 May 1951 it was a popular train, often loaded with up to thirteen coaches. Merchant Navy Class No. 35027 *Port Line* charges through the central lines at Eastleigh station. Portions from Weymouth and from Swanage were attached at Bournemouth. On summer Saturdays, to relieve the crowds wanting to use the train, a separate Swanage train ran via Wimborne avoiding Bournemouth altogether such were the numbers. (R.K. Blencowe Negative Archive)

Always planned as a temporary exhibition, the festival ran for five months before closing in September 1951. It had been a success and turned over a profit as well as being extremely popular. In the month that followed the closure however, a new Conservative government was elected to power. It is generally believed that the incoming prime minister, Churchill, considered the festival a piece of socialist propaganda, a celebration of the achievements of the Labour Party and their vision for a new socialist Britain, so the order was quickly made to level the South Bank site removing almost all trace of the 1951 festival. The only feature to remain was the Royal Festival Hall, which is now a Grade I listed building, the first post-war building to become so protected and is still hosting concerts to this day.

The role of the railways

The festival was highly popular in every part of Britain. An estimate was that of the national population of 49 million, about half participated. The festival largely ignored foreign tourists, with most of the visitors from the Continent being expatriate Britons. Most movement around the country, especially to London, was performed by trains.

Coronation of Queen Elizabeth II, 1953. Planning for the queen's coronation started more than a year before the date set aside by protocol. The one-day ceremony on 2 June 1953 took fourteen months of preparation; the first meeting of the Coronation Commission was in April 1952, under the chairmanship of the queen's husband, Prince Philip, Duke of Edinburgh. Ninety-six thousand people were planned to come to London and line the route of the approximately 5 mile long procession. Although television was in its infancy, thousands more would have attended if it had not been for the broadcast coverage (approximately 27 million people were estimated to have watched the event on television sets). It rained on part of the route. On 15 June the queen attended a review of the fleet at the Spithead at Portsmouth and a huge crowd came to witness the event, many arriving by train. Along a route lined with sailors, soldiers, and airmen and women from across the British Empire and Commonwealth, guests and officials passed in a procession before about 3 million spectators that were gathered on the streets of London, some having camped overnight in their spot to ensure a view of the monarch, and others having access to specially built stands and scaffolding along the route. For those not present, more than 200 microphones were stationed along the path and in Westminster Abbey, with 750 commentators broadcasting in 39 languages.

The procession included foreign royalty and heads of state riding to Westminster Abbey in various carriages. After the procession ended, the royal family appeared on the balcony of Buckingham Palace to watch a flypast of 168 fighter jets, which flew overhead in three divisions 30 seconds apart, at an altitude of 1,500 feet. (B.K.B. Brooksbank)

There were over 10 million paid admissions to the six main exhibitions over a period of five months. The most popular event was the centrepiece at South Bank Exhibition with almost 8.5 million visitors, over half of them from outside London. The Festival Pleasure Gardens had over 8 million visitors, three-quarters of them from London. The festival ship *Campania*, which docked in 10 cities, was visited by almost 900,000 people. The Travelling Land Exhibition, which went to four English cities, attracted under 500,000. The most specialised events, in terms of attracting few visitors, were the architecture exhibition in Poplar, with 87,000 visitors and the 63,000 who visited the exhibition of books in South Kensington.

International Railway Conference, 1954. In a remarkable similarity to events after the First World War, an exhibition of railway wares was held shortly after hostilities ceased. Willesden in North London was the site of a joint exhibition by BR, London Underground and various manufacturers.

The International Railway Congress Association is a forum for the management of the railways of the world to exchange their views and to standardise their working practices wherever desirable. It meets every four years in various host countries and the 1954 congress was in Britain. Delegates to the congress were also invited to the Rugby locomotive testing plant in May 1954. Oddly enough, photographs of this international event have proved very hard to find, hence this less than best one taken in the roundhouse. There the delegates could inspect different engines. To haul express passenger trains, BR exhibited a large Pacific locomotive. So new was this engine that the organisers played safe and had only a line drawing of No. 71000 in their booklet. However, the real thing did materialise, as exhibit No. 12, on display at Willesden. Making its appearance in 1954 from Crewe was Class 8 power classification locomotive No. 71000 received the name *Duke of Gloucester*, on the right. By this time, the writing was on the wall for steam hauled express passenger trains and so this is the only example of its class and it had a short shelf life. Also on display was an engine for pulling heavy freight trains, on the left. Perverse as it may seem with the scaling down of steam for passenger uses, that it should be in the ascendency for freight haulage, this class not appearing until 1954. This was one of BR's most successful locomotives and was probably the pinnacle of design of steam engines in Britain with 251 being built. (BPC)

CHAPTER 28
STANDARDISATION OF RAILWAY LOCOMOTIVES

With around 100 different types of steam engine the board had to contend with, the idea of centralisation on a few different types or to progress with the numerous existing models was a conundrum the board came to grips with. For a few years after the war they continued, mainly due to a lack of alternatives, to turn out locomotives to the designs of the Big Four companies. Standardisation, if it could be achieved, was seen as an effective method of reducing costs. The Big Four had, each in their own way, already been pursuing this concept within their own fleets, but the next stage, pursuing across the board was a different, and daunting prospect.

Locomotive exchange, 1948

While there was nothing new in railway companies wanting to compare their locomotives, only rail disciples would have any knowledge of trials before those in 1948. Very early into the new era, the chairman of the ME (BR), Robert A. Riddles, wrote deciding that, 'it was desirable to obtain preliminary comparison of the performance of different standard locomotives in service.' Some would say that those trials were no more than a publicity stunt so that the newly nationalised system could be shown to be doing something. Others would believe that these were genuine attempts to compare locomotive performance with a view to taking forward the best practices for the new company. All the locomotives were tender types and were placed into one of three categories: passenger, mixed traffic and freight. Without going to great expense, some locomotives were restricted from some routes for example, loading gauge and weight limitations. Prior to the trials there was a week of route familiarisation, for example there are no water troughs on the Waterloo to Exeter line. Others would say it was a waste of time given the rising tide of diesel and electric motive power. Not much resulted from the trials and it may have been better to have selected a single route and one has to ask, if one design had proved better, was it the intention of BR to go into production of older technology when standard locomotives were being thought about and at the expense of electrification.

These exchanges may be thought of as a prelude to commissioning a few slimmed down number of design that the new company was to work with, all over the system. However, this scientific approach is rather fanciful as even before the exchanges began, BR was already drawing up designs for future locomotives suggesting the experiments were largely superfluous – a good publicity stunt nevertheless. However, trainspotters relished the sight of GWR engines at Gorton (Manchester), Bulleid Pacifics at Perth

Waterloo. What a sight. One of Gresley's LNER celebrated A4 Class streamlined engines, No. 22 *Mallard*, heading out from Waterloo station bound for Exeter, on the SR. No one would believe a trainspotter if they recounted this tale at school the next day. From April to August 1948 it must have been a time of great expectations with no internet to forewarn enthusiasts. Using the evidence of the trials, the Locomotive Standards Committee were unable to recommend any one design in preference to another. If anything, they showed that route availability was paramount, favouring mixed-traffic engines. (BPC)

and Maylebone, former LNER A3s in Plymouth and Royal Scot engines at Paddington. If anything was gleaned from the trials it was that mixed traffic locomotives were preferred to specific express engines for their route and purpose availability.

Standard class engines

BR settled on a range of engines, from tank engines for lightly used lines to very powerful locomotives for pulling heavy freights. A power classification was assigned to each engine, from 2 to the most powerful, 9. With a small number of classes of locomotives they could be serviced all over the system and could be used anywhere, a marked contrast to the over 100 different designs BR inherited. However, with servicable locomotives available, the older different engines were to be relied upon for some years to come – an accountant would suggest that to give a fair return on the capital cost an engine should last between twenty-five to thirty-five years. Noticeable by their absence are small shunting engines. With success of (later Class 8) early diesel engines (both LNER and LMSR) it was felt unnecessary, and what's more, the diesels were more economical. Apart from the Britannia Class (and the unique *Duke of Gloucester*) and the Class 9 freight engines, the standard classes were labelled as, mixed traffic engines. This dual designation allowed a degree of flexibility for usage on different lines to suit the differing nature of the work available. One of the best liked was the Britannia Class. Their 6ft 2in driving wheels was a compromise for their mixed-traffic role to allow sustained fast running with passenger trains, yet small enough to give sufficient tractive effort for freight haulage.

Class 8 engine No. 71000 *Duke of Gloucester*. This unique engine had a chequered rise to publicity and a speedy birth. A gap appeared in Crewe's schedule due to the writing off of engine No. 46202 after the crash at Harrow. Easing into this space went a prototype engine in late March 1954. The finished engine was displayed at the International Railway Congress at Willsden in May and it was returned to Crewe before entered into revenue earning work in July – all rather hasty for a one-off. The engine was frequently rostered to haul the Mid-Day Scot seen here at Euston. The Caprotti valve gear shows up well. Despite, according to commentators of the day, being an excellent engine, when it was decided to electrify its stomping ground, its days were numbered, 1 December 1962 being its withdrawal date. (R.K. Blencowe)

Opposite above: **Class 5.** This class of engine the second most numerous of all the standard types (172), only the very large freight engines (Nos. 920000 plus) were more numerous. This is not surprising really as amongst the Big Four, the 4-6-0 wheel arrangement as seen in Halls (WR), B1s (LNER) and Class 5s (LMSR) totalled over 1,400 engines and so any replacement would be very numerous. In some respects, these engines are hybrids taking the best bits from other designs and merging them together; cylinders, wheels and motion similar to those on Class 6 (Clan Class) engines while the boiler was similar to the LMSR Class 5 locomotives. No. 73111 is seen here at Eastleigh. They were allocated mostly to the LMSR, twenty-three to the SR, ten to the WR and only five to the LNER. Twenty of those allocated to the SR took over names released from N15 locomotives (King Arthur Class) and the WR engines were tried with Caprotti valve gears. (RAS)

Opposite below: **Class 9.** These engines were the most numerous of all the standard class of engines, with 251 locomotives. They were nearly never built. When proposals for a standard heavy freight locomotive were being discussed then an eight wheeled version with a trailing truck under the cab rose to the top of the pile. However, following the end of the war there were numerous engines capable of fulfilling the task and with steel rationing in force, it was not a priority. After more discussion, the principle of greater hauling power, compared to existing heavy freight locomotives, became paramount. A training truck could offer nothing to the debate but an extra pair of driving wheels could. There did exist a small class of such engines (Austerities) and their performance was promising. Consequently a design with 10 coupled wheels was developed, 178 to be built at Crewe and 73 at Swindon. The last steam engine built in this country was No. 92220 *Evening Star*, at Swindon Works. The name was a result of a competition run by the staff Western Region of BR prior to the engine's completion; three workers independently came up with the same name. The plaque reads,

> No. 92220 built at Swindon
> March 1960
> The last steam locomotive for British Railways
> Named at Swindon on March 18, 1960, by
> K.W.C. Grand, Esq
> Member of the British Transport Commission

Though the last to be built, it was not the last 9F numerically as Crewe Works had already completed engines with higher numbers. In total, 999 Standard Class locomotives were built. Ten were built with a Franco-Crosti boiler. Unlike conventional boilers, the heat remaining in the exhaust gases is used to preheat the water supply for the main boiler using a secondary heat exchange mechanism. These locomotives were recognisable as they had a secondary smokebox door, below the standard one, and the exhaust chimney was on the right-hand side of the boiler. With no exhaust emitting from the standard chimney, these engines had no smoke deflectors at the front, some had a small one attached to the side exhaust. (BPC)

STANDARDISATION OF RAILWAY LOCOMOTIVES • 197

CHAPTER 29
THE RISE OF THE MOTOR CAR, PACKAGE HOLIDAYS AND MOTORWAYS

The railway's decline following the end of the Second World War was not solely due to the rise of motor transport. Earlier I have commented on the rise of small goods vehicles performing local deliveries, much the same as horse and carts had done for centuries. The flexibility of small goods vehicles and the steady stream of de-mobbed drivers saw the growth of such vehicles to 300,000 by the mid-1920s. Haulage played a particular role in changing the transportation of heavy goods – for instance cement, bricks and other aggregates – allowing large-scale building projects to happen more quickly and cheaply. Combined with increased affluence, house building sky-rocketed from around 100,000 new homes in 1925 to more than 330,000 in 1935. Regarding containers, the railways really missed a golden opportunity here. With the prospect of door to door transfers, the railways dabbled with containers but did not market them sufficiently. With containers able to be loaded at the factory and door step, the railways could have stolen a march on other firms as they had a national distribution system readily available.

Safety and regulation had become key issues, with the Heavy Goods Vehicle Speed Limit Committee of 1953 and road haulage denationalisation in the same year. Records from the mid-1950s show that other issues included licensing, railway strike action and delays at docks. The British government were trying in vain to revive the ailing railways, which were trapped by a decaying infrastructure, tight regulation of services and fares, pay disputes, and a reliance on steam and a first operating loss in 1955. The reliance of industry on rail was being eroded on all these fronts.

As a result of the Transport Act 1947, the BTC established BRS in 1948. It was the road transport company formed by the nationalisation of Britain's road haulage industry. Lorries at that time were of the rigid body type and it was not until 1964 that articulated vehicles appeared; the following year 75 per cent of heavy chassis were tractor unit/trailer type.

Motor coaches had been in operation since the First World War, their capacity, seating and range changed drastically after the Second World War. Local buses, with trams, eroded the suburban base from the railways. They were often used by companies to bring their workers to the factories. Bus companies operated by railway companies had the best of both worlds. In 1947, they made over £3.5 million profit. In this post-war period with petrol on ration, hire vehicles subject to a 20 mile radius restriction and people's desire to take trips and commute meant their revenues blossomed.

Long distance coach travel for excursions and holidays. This was nothing new, the vehicles became larger and more comfortable. The quality of roads rendered them not to everyone's liking. The revolutionary concept of having the motor under the seats was a game changer. With increased affluence, the demand for goods increased after the war. This led to new factories and car plants pulling workers away from the traditional heavy industries. Their rates of pay tended to outstrip the wages paid by railways leading to shortages. The unwillingness of their paymasters to increase wages led to disputes, especially in 1955. Some were disputes within the industry itself, which the public could not understand. As a result, traffic – goods and passengers – was diverted away from rail onto lorries and coaches. Here are a group of unskilled men with most to lose from the new factories with new skills. The 1955 rail strike started on 29 March, threatening the Whitsun bank holiday. Emphasising the crucial role of the railways in peace time was the fact that the queen had to cancel her Trooping the Colour ceremony. On advice from her ministers, the queen declared a state of emergency giving the government powers to maintain essential services and essential supplies. The railways effectively delayed introduction of the summer timetable by two weeks, until 27 June and the strike appeared to have had little effect on bulk goods (coal) movement. (BPC)

Motorways

The Roads Act 1920 created a tax on road vehicles to help with upkeep. In 1919, Parliament gave the newly-formed Ministry of Transport the power to classify roads, leading to the first road numbering system that the ministry published in 1922 and revised in 1926. The ministry took control of the core road network in 1936, and it was also during this period that the Institution of Highway Engineers and the County Surveyors' Society published their first reports and plans for high-speed road network throughout the UK, the basis for the first motorways. The very first motorway in the UK was the Preston Bypass and it was opened by Harold Macmillan, the prime minister, in 1958. It offered businesses and tourists a quicker route between the Lake District and Blackpool. The bypass is now part of the M6. The public were used to new roadworks, but the scale of these new motorways took them by surprise. Fed up with traffic jams, such innovations were well received. The first full motorway was the M1, of which the first stretch was opened in 1959. Believe it or not, motorists could drive as fast as they wanted as there was no official speed limit. The three carriageways were designed to accommodate 14,000 vehicles a day but today serves ten times that number.

It was not only the size of the new roads that delighted people but the layouts. Vehicles could just glide on and off connecting roads and some coach operators advertised trips along these new roads, and back home. In 1958 there were only 4.5 million cars in Britain. Fifty years later the figure had risen to 28 million. However, there were twice as many fatalities on the country's roads in those early days of motorways compared to today.

With regard to the 1938 proposals first of all, there were still no London-Newcastle or Portsmouth motorways, no M5 north of Birmingham and no M66 Trans-Pennine section. The 1936 proposals had motorways going all over the place, notably including

Motorway cafes. Britain's first motorway service station was Watford Gap services, which opened on the same day as the M1. Considered by many to be the dividing line between the North and South of England, the location became known as the place where touring musicians could get a break and a meal on the way to and from their gigs. It gets its name from a gap in the chalk hills around London, which leads to Watford when heading south.

Norwich and Plymouth. Unfortunately, as with most elements of transport in this country, notably rail electrification and the construction of new airports, short termism and an unwillingness to think strategically have contributed to our present sorry state. One of the first inner-city motorways was proposed in 1922 by Lord Montagu. He suggested that as it was almost impossible to widen roads in London unless tunnels or overpasses were built.

Elevated roads. This is the Chiswick flyover taking the new M4 motorway over a busy West London roundabout. Road projects always caused controversy. Motorists paid their road fund licence to the government who paid for the improvements, a bottomless pit of funds. However, rail improvements had to come out of revenue generated by the railways, putting them at a disadvantage so they thought. A new motorway should be built on viaducts, with supporting structures that could contain flats and offices. Of course, the idea of working in an office or living in a flat that supported a major motorway probably didn't sound too appealing, and the idea was quickly dropped. That did not stop Lord Montagu from proposing an even more ambitious idea – a motorway that would connect London and Liverpool. This motorway would pass through Coventry, Birmingham, Wolverhampton, Stoke-on-Trent, and Manchester. It could technically be considered as a predecessor to the M1 and M6. The road was largely supported, especially by Newcastle-under-Lyme. But there was some disinterest from the government at the time. One of its most surprising opponents was the president of the Commercial Motor Users' Association. They did not believe that motorways would be of any interest to trade vehicles. Meanwhile, much of Europe was already beginning to build their own highways. Italy opened the first motorway-like road in 1924, known as the *autostrade*. Germany, meanwhile, opened their first *autobahn* in 1932. Unsurprisingly, the outbreak of the Second World War put a hold on major road projects once again. However, the first real sign that the government was dedicated to building high speed roads came in 1949, when the Special Roads Act was approved. This act allowed the construction of roads that could prohibit the likes of pedestrians and non-motor vehicles. Work began on what would become the first motorway in the UK in 1956, a dual two-lane road to the east of Preston, which would eventually be known as the Preston Bypass. Preston was chosen as its location in the North frequently became a bottleneck for long distance traffic. This was the meeting point for those wishing to travel towards Scotland, and those wanting to holiday in Blackpool. Building the UK's first motorway here would help to alleviate the heavily congested roads. (BPC)

CHAPTER 30
THE CHANGING FACE OF BRITISH RAILWAYS
THE MOMENTOUS 1950s AND EARLY 1960s

After the First World War, the four railway companies devised programmes to upgrade and improve their systems. This they did according to the money available and the way forward to make profit as they saw things. They were strapped for cash, but the government's financial programmes came to their rescue and enabled their plans to be enacted. In rather parallel ideas, thirty years later, also after another world war, the country's railways looked for improvements to the system following nationalisation. This time, and in many people's eyes logically or not before time, a modernisation programme was devised. While the design of Standard Class locomotives had been settled upon, there were many in the top echelons of the industry who, seeing the rebuilding progress on the Continent, favoured investigation into the wholesale use of diesel and electric traction. 'Stick with what you know', was the watchword of the day. However, it was plain to see that once the restrictions of the Second World War were lifted, it wasn't to the old ways that the country wanted to return. In the early 1950s, trying to recover from the near bankruptcy caused by the war, BR pressed on with building diesel locomotives and replacing coaching stock (and smaller steam engines) with DMUs.

Diesel multiple units

The first lightweight DMUs had entered service in the Leeds area in 1954, revolutionising the services in the area and heralding in many new passengers. However, reliability was an issue with steam hauled services having to deputise. By the late 1950s, Swindon Carriage Works was already dispatching through Gloucester Carriage and Wagon Works, the first Inter-City DMUs, some driving cars of which were built with through corridor connections. They were initially introduced onto Glasgow-Edinburgh services in January 1957, with further units provided for the inauguration, on 17 June on the Swansea-Birmingham service. Early 1958 saw Swindon producing another batch of three-car cross-country DMUs for use on other services in the south-west. However, on 10 March, they took over Birmingham-South

Wales duties from the Inter-City DMUs introduced only nine months earlier. From 13 January, many local services in Newport and the Cardiff valleys were reorganised also using new three-car suburban DMUs built at Derby. Gloucester Railway Carriage and Wagon Works were also still involved in new construction for BR. A fleet of forty two-car DMUs were built for the London Midland and Scottish regions from summer 1957, the Scottish ones being introduced from 3 February 1958 on Edinburgh local services.

Warrington, 1961. A two-car lightweight unit enters the station from the south. Units such as these replaced services on branch lines (note the white 'whiskers' on the front) and consisted of two or three coaches. Being able to be driven from either end removed the previous necessity – which was very time consuming – of releasing the engine from the front and re-instating it at the rear, now the front.

Delamere, 1963. One of the important features of these new units was their versatility. This train, probably originating from Manchester Central, is at one of the stations on the Cheshire Lines Railway's service en route for Chester, Northgate. Short units could be coupled together; this train consists of two units joined together. For much of the day shorter trains sufficed and at peak periods units could be joined together. However, with many manufacturers (at least eight) there were individual differences that meant that not all units could be coupled to all other units.

Selby, 1963. Although DMUs had replaced shorter trains the concept of Inter-City trains was gathering pace. As well as those already listed, a special set of carriages were built in Swindon to form the Trans-Pennine Express trains. These consisted of six carriages, two powered driving cars, two powered buffet units and two trailer cars. Originally, they were designed to link Liverpool, Manchester, Leeds and Hull and their speed – each train had 1,840hp – meant that the timetable could be improved by shortening the timings between cities. However, insufficient trains were built so to complement these units were 2,000hp diesel hauled, ten coach trains linking Newcastle too, although the performance could not match those of the TransPennine units.

Pilot diesel locomotives

The BTC published their Modernisation Plan 'A Blueprint for the Modernisation of British Railways' in 1955. Part of this plan outlined the desire to replace steam locomotives with diesel and electrics, over a ten-year period. The BTC identified a range of power requirements and, probably under government exhortation, wishing to stimulate British industry by placed orders with a variety of companies for the production of pilot scheme locomotives for evaluation. As a result, 174 locomotives falling into four power output bands were ordered from North British Locomotive Company, Metropolitan-Vickers, BRC&W, The English Electric Company Limited, British Thomson-Houston Brush-Bagnall Traction Limited and their own workshops at Derby and Swindon.

Experimental locomotives

Deltic. Large, 100mph diesel locomotives, like the Deltic, showed that their efficiency and availability could bring about great savings. For example, under steam, the East Coast route needed fifty-five steam locomotives whereas it only required twenty-two diesel locomotives giving a glimpse of the new operating future. The first new locomotives appeared at the end of 1957 when steam engines were still being built, a complete contradiction in policy! A government White Paper, produced in 1956, stated that modernisation would help eliminate BR's financial deficit by 1962.

Other experimental locomotives

To meet the requirements of BR for a powerful locomotive with two bogies, each with three axels, *Lion* was a private venture as a substitute for the earlier (two bogie, four axle) locomotives such as the Peak classes. The specifications were revealed by the BTC at a meeting on 15 January 1960. Train heating was to be by both steam and electric train heating. Unlike the earlier pilot scheme, the BTC expected that these prototypes would be funded by the makers, rather than bulk orders being placed sight unseen. The Type 4 gave rise to three prototypes: *Falcon*, DP2 and *Lion*, which eventually led to the classes 47 and 50 locomotives. As well as BR's own works at Derby, Ashford and Swindon, several other manufacturers were involved in the process of designing and building the new diesel locomotives including The English Electric Company Limited, Brush-Bagnall Traction Limited, British Thompson-Houston, North British Locomotive Company and Metropolitan-Vickers.

However, by the mid-1950s it was apparent that parts of the rail industry were in decline. Less of the country's internal trade was favourable to rail and large parts of the network were entirely uneconomic, with BR having no idea of how to deal with it. With this as a background, BR launched its Modernisation Plan (or to give it its proper title, Modernisation and Re-Equipment of the British Railways) in 1955. Time and ideas had moved on. However, the plan invested too much in untried diesel manufacturing in the UK, at the disadvantage of electrification. The plan published in 1955 was about just that, modernisation of equipment and trains not the infrastructure or management. In the first four years of the plan, BR had invested £421 million in traction and rolling stock.

Rail Strike, 1955

The post-war boom, following the relaxation of rationing, resulted in an exodus of staff away from the railways. The lure of cleaner, better jobs and higher wages meant that those operating the railways put in demands for more money to keep pace with the foreign holidays, cars and consumer goods that their once fellow workers were now able to command. Jobs on the railways were usually manual, and involved working outside and getting dirty. These men typify the mind set of the day; older, male dominated and few amenities, and working in all weathers. The railways had an aging, unskilled labourforce at a time when the industry needed younger, skilled staff.

New trades. Many workers moved to production line jobs. Although the drive to improve the skill base of the employees was gathering pace with technical schools and the like, most workers had only a school leaving certificate. An aptitude test got them a job in the factory; boring, repetitive it may have been, but it was better paid. The 1950s was an era of great house building, the government of the day wanted to build 1 million a year. Of course men to build them had to come from somewhere – the railways. More men were trained in the skills necessary to build houses. They not only had higher wages but became skilled rather than just labourers. 'Never had it so good', was the slogan used by Harold Macmillan as prime minister in 1957. (BPC)

Clean Air Act 1956. Due to a series of dense mist/fogs – smog – in the early part of December 1952, the atmospheric conditions created a 'lid' over central London, leading to a four-day deadly emergency with over 4,000 people dying. The 'lid' kept the exhausts from the nine coal fired power stations in London from escaping into the atmosphere and it became so bad that cars, lorries and buses were simply abandoned on the roadside. The government considered this situation a price for our industrial wealth. They encouraged the export of good quality coal and took low quality 'nutty slack' off ration. This 1950s shot is of a couple trying to filter the air they breathed. In 1953, doctors were able to prescribe masks made with pads of gauze or cotton wool, costing a shilling. The BMA regarded them as temporary measures and looked forward to the day when legistation made their use in 'pea-soupers' unecessary. One big contributor, in built up areas, was the exhausts from steam engines. Certain fuels, called 'smokeless fuels' became available, but with power stations increasing in number and motor vehicles as well, the government introduced legislation in 1956. (BPC)

Modernisation in practice. Omlettes and eggs spring to mind when looking at this picture of Manchester London Road. This view shows the station throat, especially the South Junction side. In the background is signal box A with it bomb protective flat roof and to the right are the viaduct lines heading south. On the left is ex-GCR signal box C. The platform ends below our position are for trains from the Altrincham/Ordsall Lane direction actually well above Manchester's street. To the right of the string of wagons for the removal of debris, are the remains of platform ends and a turntable for the Altrincham trains. Class 5 engine No. 44833 may well be using the joint line platforms as its normal ones, in the main station, are undergoing alteration to accommodate electric trains. (BPC)

There was also a demand for office trained workers usually women. Grammar schools had a balance of the sexes in their makeup and better skilled women were produced; no longer was it the role of women to mind the home and children but their extra wages, from cleaner office jobs and not just factory work, enabled those yearned-for goods to be bought, one of which would be a car. The rise of usage of motor vehicles had a profound effect on the way the nation moved. An appraisal of the nation's railway lines showed that the network in the mid-1950s differed little from that inherited nearly forty years previously. However, more passengers went by car (war time petrol rationing continued until 1953) and goods went by larger lorries, both cutting into the railway's financial structure. Consequentlly, the commission launched its Modernisation Plan in 1955 which would put the industry on an even keel in fifteen years time. Five years later and new construction of steam locomotives ceased and the wholesale use of DMUs began to carry more passengers. (BPC)

New engines

One of the main line routes for electrification was that between London (Euston) and Liverpool/Manchester.

A Class locomotive No. E3033. The first section to be opened was from Crewe to Manchester, in 1960. At 3,300hp these were more powerful than the largest Coronation Pacifics on the LMSR, without the smoke and grime. However, less regard was given to a comprehensive view regarding the movement of freight. Whilst larger wagons were introduced, larger handling facilities were built and marshalling yards were constructed, the competition from road traffic was the dealth knell. With better quality roads, and the onset of motorways, then factory to door concepts could be offered to customers and it saw the development of delivery fleets. The concepts that attracted freight to the roads BRS also worked for passengers, especially summer holiday traffic, the holiday passenger traffic of the latter years of the 1950s would be their nadir.

CHAPTER 31
NEW DIESEL LOCOMOTIVES

The early 1950s saw a rush, with indecent haste, to not only eliminate steam from the system but to embrace many untried diesel locomotives. The descision to have diesel hydraulic engines and others were examples of the board wanting instant results, ordering large numbers of models based on very little experience. In the early years after BR was created, steam locomotion was considered to be the prime mover of people and goods. To some extent, BR's management wallowed behind their review of steam locomotives and their standard class of locomotives. It was thought that this would be sufficient until enough money and plans warranted the wholesale shift to diesel and electric traction. Apart from a growing selection of diesel shunters, there had been almost no development of main

Warship Class locomotives, Totnes, 1961. The first of the new breed of diesel locomotives ordered through the Modernisation Plan, No. D8000 emerged from The English Electric Company Limited at Newton-le-Willows on 18 June 1957. They were complemented by the No. D800 series of hydraulics, under construction at Swindon from May 1957, although the first of the class was not released until 14 July 1958, when No. D800 was named *Sir Brian Robertson*. The first of a further class of Type 2 diesel-hydraulics for the WR in the D6300–D6357 series built by North British Locomotive Company appeared in January 1959. Production of this class was slow, and they only started to appear on running-in turns from Swindon in autumn 1959. They later joined their big sisters in Devon and Cornwall. By November 1959, passenger services in Devon and Cornwall had been handed over entirely to diesels. About to enter Totness are two diesels, No. D831 *Monach* being led by a North British Locomotive Company hydraulic engine.

line diesel or electric traction beyond the few locomotives ordered by the Big Four companies.

As ever, the plans of BR changed, leading to the Modernisation Plan of 1955. The emphasis was on wholesale dieselisation to replace steam locomotion, ignoring the fact that some of the most modern steam locomotives were efficient and were just being built. No stopgap until electrification emerged with events in the late 1950s and early 1960s reflecting this changeable situation.

The Modernisation Plan encompassed a large range of constructions from shunters to heavy express-passenger and freight locomotives, as well as DMUs. Such was BR's haste to implement the plan that a wide variety of designs from a number of their own workshops and private locomotive builders was instigated.

In the early period of BR, steam locomotion had continued to be of prime importance, indeed, the decision was taken to re-equip with steam rather than to seek alternative traction methods, in some respects the situation was similar to that after the First World War when faced with a need for new motive power, it was safer to opt for established practices rather than to back a relatively untried alternative. However, following the cessation of building steam locomotives in 1960, and the development of DMUs as well as the piecemeal construction of some main line locomotives led to the development of trial locomotives.

The 1955 Modernisation Plan heralded big changes in this situation, and from 1957 a new numbering system was used for diesel and electric locomotives ordered by BR, including those shunters ordered before 1957, which were renumbered into the new system. All steam and gas-turbine locomotives and diesel and electric locomotives built to pre-nationalisation orders retained their existing numbers under the 1948 arrangements, though some had a D or E prefix added to their number in error.

First Generation Diesel Locomotives

BR used engine power output to categorise the new main line diesel locomotive fleet following the 1955 Modernisation Plan. Shunting locomotives, from 300 to 799hp were simply designated as shunters (numbers D2000 to 4999). Type 1 was for power output 800 to 1,000hp; Type 2 for 1,001 to 1,499hp; Type 3 for 1,500 to 1,999hp; Type 4 for 2,000 to 2,999hp; and Type 5 for 3,000hp or greater. The prefix D persisted until the last main line steam locomotive was withdrawn in August 1968.

BR's Modernisation Plan of the 1950s started, sensibly, with small orders for a variety of diesel locomotives, intended for different purposes, from a range of manufacturers including its own workshops at Swindon and Derby. This was the pilot scheme, and the idea was to analyse the reliability and performance of these 174 locomotives of 14 types in service before placing larger orders. Unfortunately, in its haste to eradicate steam traction, the railway then ordered large quantities of many of these designs before they had been thoroughly tested; this resulted in failures, early withdrawals and even the re-equipping of one large class with new engines at great expense and inconvenience. Some of the designs (for example, some of the classes 20s and 26s), however, were ultimately successful and perpetuated, lasting in service until the 1990s in some cases. The railway itself was not fully prepared for its expensive new toys, and the new diesels had to share facilities with steam locomotives – not an ideal environment for such temperamental machines.

Type 1

No. D9517 at Bristol, 1966. Illustrating their prime purpose is this engine hauling a trip freight from one year to another. Note the large number of wagons and the goods shed in the background. However, this was a market and venues that were in steep decline. As their purpose declined so did the need for such locomotives and within a few years they were all withdrawn from service. This engine was one of a small group of diesel hydraulic engines built by BR at their Swindon workshops built in the mid-1960s. The good all-round visibility from the cab and dual controls also made them capable of being used for shunting duties. The order was expanded from twenty-six to fifty-six in mid-1963, before work had started on the first order. They were numbered D9500–D9555. Originally all were allocated to depots on the Western Region of BR but in January 1967 twenty were sent to Hull to work in the dockyards followed by thirteen more later the same year. At Hull they were intended for work around the docks, but the tasks were beyond the capabilities of a single locomotive; and since two locomotives required two sets of crew, they were not popular with the region. In 1968, all thirty-three ER locomotives were placed in storage, and were subsequently withdrawn on 1 April of that year. The class, like many other early diesel types, had an extremely short life with BR – in this case not because of poor reliability, but because many of its envisaged duties disappeared on the BR network a few years after they came into use. The entire class had been sold to industry or scrapped by the end of 1970. In their new careers in industry, many had a working life two to three times longer than that with BR. The industries in which they were employed, such as coal mining, declined during the 1970s and the class again became surplus to requirements.

Type 1

No. D8084 at Springburn, Glasgow. This class of diesel-electric locomotives, 228 in total, were built by The English Electric Company Limited between 1957 and 1968, the large number being in part because of the failure of other early designs in the same power range to provide reliable locomotives. The locomotives were originally numbered D8000–D8199 and D8300–D8327. Designed to work light mixed traffic, they had no train heating facilities. Locomotives up to No. D8127 were fitted with disc indicators in the style of the steam era; when headcodes were introduced in 1960 the locomotive's design was changed to incorporate headcode boxes. Although older locomotives were not retrofitted with headcode boxes, a few of the earlier batch acquired headcode boxes as a result of repairs. Unusually for British designs, the locomotive had a single cab. This caused serious problems with visibility when travelling nose first, though in these circumstances the driver's view is comparable to that on the steam that the Class 20s replaced. It was common, however, to find Class 20s paired together at the nose, with their cabs at opposite ends, ensuring that the driver could quite clearly see the track ahead, and a guard can watch the train from the other locomotive without the need for a brake van.

The Class 20 saw only limited service on passenger trains. A small number were fitted with a through pipe for steam heating, primarily for use in conjunction with other locomotive on the West Highland Line. Otherwise, their use was limited to summer relief services, particularly to Skegness, often under the adopted title of The Jolly Fisherman starting from various places in the Midlands including, Burton-on-Trent, Stoke-on-Trent, Derby and Leicester as well as sometimes to other holiday resorts on the East Coast of England, also occasional duties as a pilot, and short distance diversions of electrically hauled trains over non-electrified lines. The shift of light mixed freight to the road network left BR with an oversupply of small locomotives. These Type 1s however, could work in multiple and so handle heavier traffic. Most spent the majority of their working lives coupled nose to nose in pairs to provide a more useful 2,000hp (1,500kW) unit and to solve the visibility problems.

Type 2

Arriving into platform 6 at Manchester Central in 1960 are the typical arrangement for the use of these engines-in pairs, here D5706 leads. Co-Bo 20 built 1959, No. D5700 plus. These were commonly known as known as Metrovicks, Crossleys or Co-Bos, and were built under the pilot scheme for diesel locomotives as part of the Modernisation Plan. These Crossley-engine locomotives were one of two designs built under the scheme to use two-stroke diesel engines, the other being the Baby Deltic locomotives, numbered in the D5900–D5909 series.

The locomotives had a Co-Bo wheel arrangement (a 6-wheel bogie at one end, a 4-wheel bogie at the other) – unique in BR practice and uncommon in other countries. Work had begun on the pilot scheme in 1954 and the first plan for 174 locomotives (all classes) had been produced by October, including twenty of these Metrovick Type B locomotives, although orders were not placed until November 1955.

All twenty were initially allocated to BR's London Midland Region, where they were often used in pairs on the overnight London to Glasgow Condor express freight service. After the 1961 refurbishment, they were all transferred to the Barrow-in-Furness depot (code 12E). They were withdrawn after only eleven years at work and in service.

Despite the electrical and mechanical equipment being reliable, the Crossley engines were still giving problems. A quotation was obtained by BR from The English Electric Company Limited for re-engining with an up-rated version of the reliable 8SVT prime mover, already proven in the Type 2, and this was close to proceeding. However, the entire class, along with other small non-standard diesel classes, was withdrawn from service during 1967–68, and all but one were scrapped by the end of 1969. Their parts had been sold to make new metals by the end of 1971.

Type 3

No. D6848 after construction at The Vulcan Foundry Limited, Newton-le-Willows in 1962. As part of the plan, a need was seen for a number of Type 3 locomotives, within the 1,500 to 1,999hp range. The English Electric Company Limited had already been successful with orders for types 1 and 4 diesels and had produced locomotives of similar power for railways in East Africa. A design based on the exported locomotives was put forward and accepted, a general purpose locomotive which initially found service in BR's Eastern Region. BR placed an order for forty-two Class 37 locomotives in January 1959. The first entered service on 2 December 1960. BR had ordered further Class 37s before the last of the original batch had been completed in mid-1962. The 309 locomotives produced in total were originally numbered in the range D6700–D6999 and D6600–D6608 and were nicknamed Tractors due to the unmistakable exhaust sound.

Type 4

No. D4, *Great Gable*, photographed in 1961. Partially inspired by the LMSR prototype locomotive (seen earlier on the cusp of nationalisation) No. 10000 and by SR's locomotives (Nos. 10201, 10202 and 10203) the Type 4 diesels were some of the first big diesels commissioned for the BR modernisation project and were the precursors to the classes 45 and 46 locomotives of similar design. They were originally designed to have two bogies, each with three driving axles, but it proved impossible to keep below the 20-ton axle loading limit imposed by BR civil engineers. The design of the SR series was adopted instead. Construction began in the summer of 1958; it took around nine months before first example was completed in April 1959. They were built at BR's Derby Works and were intended for express passenger services. Originally numbered D1–D10 and named after British mountains, they became known as Peaks being used on the West Coast Main Line. This example ended up at the Midland Railway Centre at Ripley.

Hydraulics on the Western Region

Type 4, Westerns, D1000–D1073. When switching to diesel traction as part of the plan of the 1950s, BR designed, and commissioned designs for a large number of locomotive types. At this time, BR's regions had a high degree of autonomy, extending as far as classes of locomotives ordered and even the design criteria for those locomotives.

Whilst almost all other diesel locomotives were diesel-electric, the Western Region employed a policy of using diesel-hydraulic traction, originally commissioning three classes of main line locomotives: a Type 2 and two Type 4s, which were built between 1961 and 1964. With pressure to increase the speed of the transition from steam to diesel, volume orders for the Type 2 and Type 4 followed in 1957, a mere two years after the original orders and well before any idea of performance or reliability could be gained, which prompted a further order, in 1961, for seventy-four diesel-hydraulics of 2,700hp (2,000kW); so when the first locomotive was outshopped from Swindon Works in December 1961, less than a year after the order was placed, the Westerns were born.

The diesel hydraulic technology was proven in Continental Europe, particularly Germany, but was new to the UK. At the time, it was considered politically unacceptable for the UK government to order railway rolling stock from foreign companies, especially German companies so soon after the Second World War. This resulted in most of the engines and transmissions being manufactured in the UK under license from the German manufacturers.

Type 3, Hymeks, No. D7089 at Didcot, 1963. In total, 101 were built between 1961–64 by Beyer, Peacock and Company at their East Manchester Works: the origin of many steam engines especially for the GCR. These locomotives were originally intended to replace steam hauled parcels and freight services in much of the Western Region as well as passenger trains around Bristol, Paddington and Hereford. They also became rostered on services in other parts of the Western Region, on expresses to South Wales (seen here). However, such duties were beyond the Type 3 engines and they were replaced by the Type 4 Western locomotives on such services, leading to accelerated timings. In later years, being classified as, non-standard led to their rationalisation in a move reminiscent of the railway's approach to steam engines.

Total Operations Processing System (TOPS)

The TOPS system is a computerised system used to keep track of a locomotive/rolling stock's location and servicing requirements. This was a computerised system developed in America to enable the railways to track their rolling stock remotely. It was adopted here in the UK in the mid-1960s in an attempt by BR to become more efficient. Implementation of the system resulted in all of BR's locomotives being renumbered to a format that the computer system could cope with. The new five-digit locomotive numbers consisted of a two-digit class number followed by a unique three-digit engine identification number.

Modernisation plan: success or failure

Massive investments were made in marshalling yards at a time when the small wagonload traffic with which they dealt was in steep decline and being lost rapidly to the roads. The Modernisation Plan called for the rapid and large-scale introduction of diesel locomotives – a total of 2,500 locomotives to be procured in 10 years at a cost of £345 million. With political considerations all but requiring that all these locomotives be built by British firms, the scope of this project was beyond the existing capacity of the British locomotive industry. This led to many designs being submitted, and accepted, from manufacturers with little or no direct experience in main-line locomotive construction. Accepting orders from myriad manufacturers also led to BR acquiring an unnecessarily diverse locomotive fleet, with large numbers of different but similar classes. This increased the cost and complexity of maintenance and led to operational difficulties (for instance there was no universal system for multiple working). The poor reliability of many of the locomotive designs procured under the Modernisation Plan led to much lower availability ratings than predicted and the large-scale withdrawal of several classes or the curtailing of planned orders, leaving BR short of suitable motive power in some areas. Some of the diesel classes ordered in 1955 were withdrawn before the steam locomotives they were intended to replace. However, most railway historians now regard it as a costly failure and a missed opportunity; an attempt was made to simply update the railways as they already stood, rather than reacting to changes in the way goods and people were travelling in the post-war years.

CHAPTER 32
THE ARRIVAL OF DR BEECHING

Beeching Report arrived in 1963. Although villified by the press and public, there were elements of Richard Beeching's plan to increase the efficiency of the nationalised railway system that had merit. There were actually two reports. The one that the popular press latched onto was The Reshaping of British Railways, which was published in 1963 and had an objective stemming the large losses being incurred during a period of increasing competition from road transport and reducing the rail subsidies necessary to keep the network running. The second report, The Development of the Major Railway Trunk Routes, was published in 1965. The first report identified 2,363 stations and 5,000 miles of railway line for closure, amounting to 55 per cent of stations, 30 per cent of route miles, and 67,700 BR positions. The second report identified a small number of major routes for significant investment. The 1963 report also recommended some less well-publicised changes, including a switch to the now-standard practice of containerisation for rail freight, and the replacement of some services with integrated bus services linked to the remaining railheads.

Mini. While this picture is of a car destined to be iconic, the whole decade was characterised by many white goods started to be mass produced as the population became more affluent. This in turn encouraged factories with their better and cleaner working conditions to emerge. This led to increased productivity and the extra wages were spent on motor cars. It was also when Cliff Richard had his first number 1 hit, *Living Doll*, postcodes were introduced as an experiment in Norwich, the Mini car was launched and the first section of the M1 had been opened a year earlier. Reconstruction had been the word following the ending of the Second World War, now revolution was the buzzword. Soon, steam would be replaced by diesels engines and Dr Beeching would investigate and present his report to the Conservative politicians of the day. (BPC)

Beyond Beeching

After two years of research, Beeching published the results of a survey of traffic on the railways. The basic conclusion was that greater part of the system was uneconomic. In around half of the area the density of traffic was so low as to unable to cover the cost of the track and signalling, adding nothing for running the stock and staff. One half of the stations produced only 2 per cent of the passenger receipts, with half of the wagons surplus to requirements. On the other hand, the other half of the system earned enough to cover the costs of the route, six times over.

The unpalatable truth of the matter that if the railways were to be made to pay their way rather than relying on subsidy, then those contributing least would have to close, and efforts concentrated on industrial lines as well as between large cities. Needless to say, the government of the day, with its zeal for profitability, eagerly embraced the findings and quickly executed them. By the end of the decade, the number of locomotives was reduced by nearly two-thirds, passenger coaches by approaching half, route mileage by one-third and staff by one half. On the positive side, electrification of the main line between London, and Liverpool and Manchester resulted in a speeding up of journey times by one third, switching from wagonloads to trainloads, leading to merry-go-round trains for bulky business like coal improved business. Steam was phased out, with indecent haste according to many. All this was achieved against a backdrop of increasing car ownership and usage as well as increasing plane travel.

The 1963 traffic survey. 1963 traffic survey. The darker the line the denser the traffic. Needless to say, the more rural parts of the country, Wales, most of Scotland, East Anglia and most of southern England made little contribution to the industry's finances. It was the heavily industrialised areas, such as South Wales, the North East, the Midlands and the Liverpool-Manchester and Leeds-Sheffield areas carting most traffic.

The results of the Beeching survey of freight traffic. From The Reshaping of British Railways, Part I. *Reproduced by permission of the Controller of Her Majesty's Stationery Office.*

SELECT BIBLIOGRAPHY

Bonavia, Michael R., *A History of the LNER*, George Allen & Unwin, 1982
Bonavia, Michael R., *The History of the Southern Railway*, Unwin Hyman, 1987.
Crump, Norman, *By Rail To Victory*, The North Eastern Railway, 1947.
Holland, Julian, *Golden Years of Rail Travel*, Times Books, 2019.
Nash, George C., *The LMS at War*, The London Midland and Scottish Railway, 1946.
Nock O.S., *A History of the LMS*, George Allen & Unwin, 1982
Quick, Michael, *Railway Passenger Stations in Great Britain*, Railway and Canal Historical Society, 2009.
Semmens, Peter, *History of the Great Western Railway*, George Allen & Unwin, 1985
Woodley, Richard, *The Day of The Holiday Express*, Ian Allan Publishing, 1996.

As can be imagined that over such a wide ranging topic and time span that a large number of book and magazines will have been consulted. Numerous people are the unprinted resource that I've chatted to and consulted, sometimes with differing views on the course of actions and the outcomes of railway policy. And then there's the politics of the events, especially since World War Two, just to muddy the water.

GLOSSARY

°	Degree
2	Squared
AEC	Associated Equipment Company
AC	Alternating Current
ARP	Air Raid Precautions
bhp	Brake Horsepower
BPC.	Bob Pixton Collection
BR	British Railways (traded as British Rail from 1965)
BRC&W	Birmingham Railway Carriage and Wagon Company
BRS	British Road Services
BTC	British Transport Commission
cc	Cubic Centimetre
CLR	Central London Railway
CME	Chief Mechanical Engineer
CR	Caledonian Railway
DC	Direct Current
DMU	Diesel Multiple Unit
ECJS	East Coast Joint Stock
EMU	Electric Multiple Unit
ft	Feet
GCR	Great Central Railway
GER	Great Eastern Railway
GNR	Great Northern Railway
GWR	Great Western Railway
G&SWR	Glasgow and South Western Railway
hp	Horsepower
HR	Highland Railway
H&BR	Hull and Barnsley Railway
in	Inch
in2	Inch Squared
KCB	Knight Commander of the Order of the Bath
km	Kilometre
km/h	Kilometre Per Hour
kV	Kilovolt
kVAC	Kilovolt Alternating Current
kVDC	Kilovolt Direct Current
kW	Kilowatt
lb	Pound
lb/in2	Pound Per Square Inch
LB&SCR	London, Brighton and South Coast Railway
LD&ECR	Lancashire, Derbyshire and East Coast Railway
LMI	Leeds Mechanics' Institute

LMR	London Midland Railway
LMSR	London, Midland and Scottish Railway
LNER	London and North Eastern Railway
LNWR	London and North Western Railway
LPTB	London Passenger Transport Board
LR	London Railway
LSWR	London and South Western Railway
LT	London Transport
L&YR	Lancashire and Yorkshire Railway
m	Metre
MCCW	Metropolitan Cammell and Wagon Company (later known as the Metro-Cammell)
mph	Miles Per Hour
MR	Midland Railway
MSJ&AR	Manchester South Junction and Altrincham Railway
MS&LR	Manchester, Sheffield and Lincolnshire Railway
M&CR	Maryport and Carlisle Railway
M&GNJR	Midland and Great Northern Joint Railway
NBR	North British Railway
NER	North Eastern Railway
NSR	North Staffordshire Railway
RAF	Royal Air Force
RAS	Railway Air Services
RCA	Railway Clerks' Association
REC	Railway Executive Committee
ROF	Royal Ordinance Factories
RTC	Railway Technical Committee
R&CHS	Railway and Canal Historical Society
SAR	Stratford-on-Avon Railway (later known as Stratford-upon-Avon) Railway
SE&CR	South Eastern and Chatham Railway
S&DJR	Somerset and Dorset Joint Railway
S&DR	Stockton and Darlington Railway
SR	Southern Railway
TOPS	Total Operations Processing System
TUC	Trades Union Congress
TVR	Taff Valley Railway
USATC	United States Army Transportation Corps
V	Volt
VAC	Volt Alternating Current
VDC	Volt Direct Current
WD	War Department
WI	Women's Institute
WR	Wirral Railway
W&KR	Wolverhampton and Kingswinford Railway

INDEX

Air raid (WW1): WW2: 14/14, 161-6
Air traffic: 137
Alternative to Grouping: 25
Armaments: 19
Ashton under Lyne: 20

Banbury yard: 56
Bevan boys: 178
Big Four: 26-9
Bristolian:10
British Empire Exhibition: 32
British Road Services: 186

Call up: 17
Cambrian Coast Express: 10
Camping coaches: 107-9
Cannon Street, Hull: 21
Cannon Street: 51
Cars/lorries/buses: 67-9
Castle class: 83
Chessington: 52
Churchill/Atlee: 164/187
Coronation QE II: 11,192

Deal Street, Manchester: 48
Diesel locomotive 10000: 181
Diesel shunters: 75
DMU: 202/4
Down Street: 154
Dr. Beeching: 218-220
Dynamotor cars: 37

East coast main line: 50
Economic conditions of 1920s: 41
Electric locomotives: 185
Evacuation: 156/9, 175

Festival of Britain: 188
Festival of Britain: 33
Flying Scotsman: 135, 6, 88, 33
Football supporters: 9

Garrett engines: 80
General Strike: 39/40, 103+
Goring troughs: 7
GWR diesels: 72-4
GWR electrification: 140

Holiday camps: 125-131
Holiday venues: 111-122

Ian Allen ABC: 70
Ilford flyover: 49
International Railway Conference, 1954: 193

Jellico specials: 17

King Class: 84
King George V: 45

L&Y railway: 10,20
Legislation 1929: 42
Line closures in 30s: 138
Loc. Trials: 38
Loco. visits abroad: 36, 103
Locomotive exchanges: 35/6, 194
Locomotive exchanges: 35-6, 194
Locomotives, LNER 04, 145,
London Bridge: 59
Lord Nelson: 85

Man. Sheff. Wath electrics: 63-5
Manchester Exchange: 70
March, shed, yard, coaling tower: 53-55
Milford tunnel:47
Mirfield: 47/8
Modernisation: 207
Motor van: 10
Motorways/coaches: 198-201
MSJ&AR: 66

Named trains: 10
Named trains: 132-135
Named trains:10
Nationalisation: 182
New Brighton: 62
New Diesel locomotives: 209-217
New lines in WW2: 172-174
New locomotives: 146-153

Old Trafford station: 66
Outside the Grouping: 23

Paddington station: 11,42
Parkston Quay: 57
Personalities: 30-1
Petersfield: 60
Pilot diesels: 205
Post WW2 named trains: 191
Princess Royal class: 87

Rail strike: (39/40), 206
Railway Executive Committee: 23, 155
Risley: 170/1
Royal Ordnance Factories: 167-169
Royal Scot tour: 36, 103-6
Royal Scot:86

S&D centenary: 34/5
Sankey sidings: 171
Seven tunnel (junction/station): 77-9
Six wheeled coaches: 110,
SR electric units: 59
Standardisation of locomotives: 194-7
Stanier 8F: 81
Static testing tables: 37
Streamlined locomotives: 89-03
Streamlined trains: 94-100
Surbiton: 61
Sutton station: 8

Taunton: 44
The Big Four: 22
Tollerton: 50
Tyneside units: 63

Underground: 141-4

War memorials: 22
Welwyn: 50
Westbury By-pass: 43, 45
Wombourne :46
Women at Work: 18, 176/7
Women at work: 18, 168/9, 179
Woodhead tunnel: 189/90

Yorkshire venues: 123/4